BEYOND BOUNDARIES

Where Ego Ends, the Mind Bends

Compiled, Crafted and Curated By

DR. HARI CHINTHAKUNTA

Copyright © Dr. Hari Chinthakunta 2025
All Rights Reserved.

ISBN
Paperback 979-8-89777-262-9
Hardcase 979-8-89906-296-4

This book has been published with all efforts taken to make the material error-free after the consent of the author. However, the author and the publisher do not assume and hereby disclaim any liability to any party for any loss, damage, or disruption caused by errors or omissions, whether such errors or omissions result from negligence, accident, or any other cause.

While every effort has been made to avoid any mistake or omission, this publication is being sold on the condition and understanding that neither the author nor the publishers or printers would be liable in any manner to any person by reason of any mistake or omission in this publication or for any action taken or omitted to be taken or advice rendered or accepted on the basis of this work. For any defect in printing or binding the publishers will be liable only to replace the defective copy by another copy of this work then available.

Beyond Boundaries

Where Ego Ends, the Mind Bends.

Sri Sri Sri Vidya Narayana Thirtha Swamyji
Dwaraka Badirikashram, Bengaluru

Interpretation of PEARLS OF WISDOM

of His Holiness Sri Vidya Narayana Thirtha

Sri Jagadguru Shankaracharya Samsthanam,

Dwaraka Badarikashram, and Sri Vidya Narayana Foundation, Bangalore

Compiled, Crafted, and Curated by

Dr. Hari Chinthakunta

With Divine Grace and Blessings from His Holiness Sri Vidyanarayana Thirtha

A Humble Dedication

At the Lotus Feet of the Eternal Guide: A Humble Dedication to the Mystic Circle of Divinity.

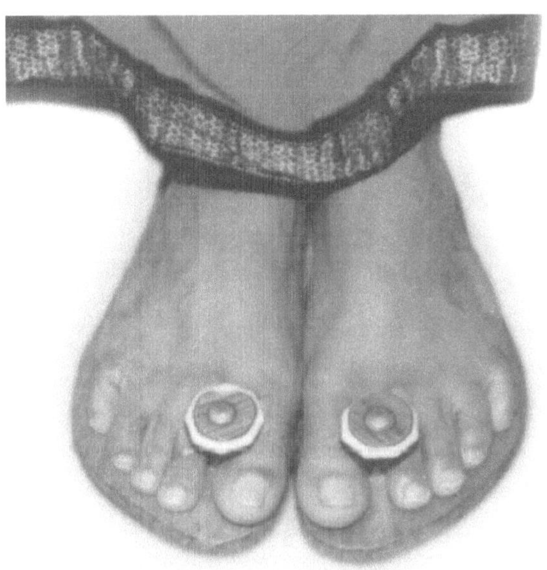

His Holiness Sri Vidya Narayana Thirtha

Sri Jagadguru Shankaracharya Samsthanam,

Dwaraka Badarikashram, and Sri Vidya Narayana Foundation, Bangalore

Contents

Breaking Conditioned Patterns

The Surrendered Mind

Beyond Fear and Desire

Silence as the Gateway

Dissolving the Self-

Walking the Pathless Path

The Vastness Within

Living Beyond Boundaries

Acknowledgements

With profound reverence, I bow before **Lord Vinayaka**, seeking His divine blessings to remove the illusions of ego and open the doors to truth. To **Lord Subramanyeswara**, I offer my prayers for the strength to transcend limitations and embrace the boundless expanse of spiritual wisdom.

I surrender at the feet of **Goddess Bala Tripura Sundari**, the eternal Mother who dissolves the false self and reveals the infinite truth. Her grace is the guiding force that leads the seeker beyond the confines of identity and into the vastness of divine realization. To **Lord Venkateshwara**, I seek the courage to walk this path with unwavering devotion, allowing truth to unfold in its highest form.

My heartfelt gratitude extends to the **Saints, Sages, and Seers** whose sacred wisdom has guided seekers throughout time. Their teachings are the bridges that carry us beyond

boundaries—beyond the ego, beyond the known, into the infinite realm of truth.

I am forever indebted to my **divine parents, Avadootha Nanna and Karunamayi Amma**, whose love has been my anchor and my guiding light. I also extend my deepest appreciation to my **divine sister, Sai Niveditha, and my brothers, Naga Yogi Raj and Balayogi Ganesh**, for their unwavering support and presence on this journey.

His Holiness Sri Vidyanarayana Theertha Swamy has dedicated fifty years to the path of sanyasa, living a life of deep wisdom and renunciation. Through his journey, he has met people from all walks of life, adapting to different situations without ever straying from the core principles of dharma. No matter the circumstances—whether facing hardships or moments of ease—Swamiji has remained steadfast, treating everyone with the same compassion and respect, free from

distinctions of caste, creed, or status.

Simplicity and independence define his way of life. He seeks nothing for himself, yet gives endlessly to those who come to him for guidance. His kindness is not

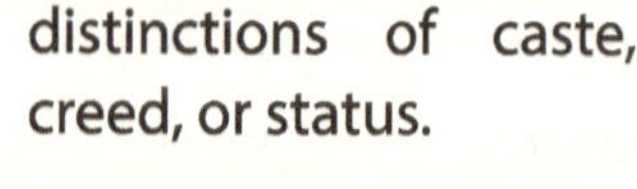

just seen but felt, as he nurtures his devotees with love and wisdom. Swamiji's life teaches that true happiness does not come from material pursuits but from embracing contentment and inner peace. His presence is a reminder that detachment and love can go hand in hand— where one expects nothing but gives everything.

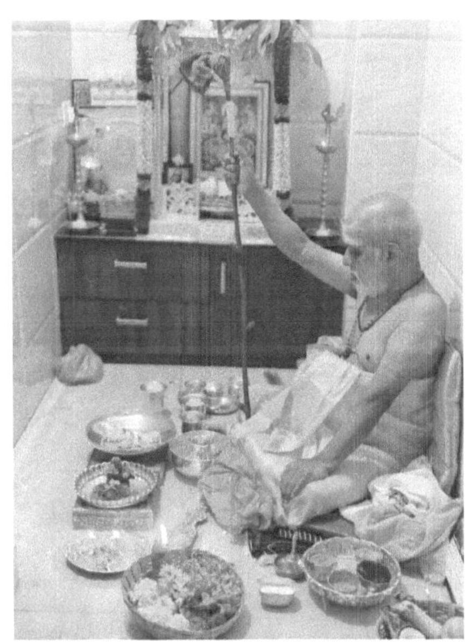

This work is a humble tribute to his grace. Swamiji has shown that the greatest journey is not one of traveling across the world but of looking within. True wisdom is not about gathering knowledge, but about surrender— letting go of the ego so that the deeper truth of existence can shine through. His life is a guiding light, showing us that real freedom comes not from having more, but from needing less, until only truth remains.

His Holiness Sri Vidyanarayana Theertha Swamy stands as a beacon of wisdom, embodying a life of profound renunciation and unwavering spiritual discipline. For five decades, he has walked the path of sannyasa, embracing both the trials and triumphs of life with grace and resilience. Through countless encounters with people from all backgrounds, he has remained steadfast— adapting to changing circumstances without ever compromising the fundamental principles of dharma. Swamiji treats all devotees alike, transcending barriers of caste, creed, and worldly distinctions, offering his guidance with unbounded compassion.

At the heart of his life is simplicity—an independence that is not just physical but deeply spiritual. Swamiji does not seek grandeur or recognition; his greatest wealth lies in his unwavering commitment to truth and selflessness. His kindness is not just an expression but

a living force, nurturing those who seek his guidance. To be in his presence is to witness a rare blend of detachment and love—where he expects nothing yet gives everything.

This work is not merely a composition but an offering shaped by his divine grace. Swamiji's presence has illuminated a truth often overlooked—the journey beyond boundaries is not one of outward exploration but of inward dissolution. True wisdom does not reside in accumulation but in surrender. Where the ego dissolves, the infinite is revealed. In Swamiji's life, we find the path to simplicity, contentment, and the ultimate realization that liberation lies not in seeking more but in becoming less—until only truth remains.

This book is an offering of that wisdom—an invitation for seekers to look beyond their perceived limitations and experience the vast, boundless reality that lies beyond the self. May it serve as a reminder that the only walls that exist are the ones we build within our own minds, and the only truth worth seeking is the one that dissolves all separation.

I extend my sincere gratitude to **Sree Lekha and Sai Leela**, whose steadfast encouragement has strengthened me in this endeavour. My heartfelt appreciation also goes to **Mrs. Konanki Lakshmi Kala**, whose keen eye for detail has helped shape this book with clarity and precision.

A special tribute is due to **Bhagwan Sri Ram SIR**, a mentor whose presence has guided me beyond the confines of conditioned thought. His wisdom has been a beacon of light, showing me that true transformation lies in transcending the self and surrendering to the boundless truth.

With infinite love and gratitude,

– Dr. Hari Chinthakunta

In the Presence of Swamy: A Journey Beyond Words

Whispers of Eternal Wisdom

There are moments in life when words transcend their ordinary meaning, becoming luminous guides to a deeper truth. Such was my experience with His Holiness Sri Vidyanarayana Theertha, whose wisdom was not just spoken—it was *alive*. His teachings were not mere concepts; they carried the power to dissolve illusions, to shift perspectives, and to awaken the spirit.

It was during my visit to Bangalore in December 2024 that Swamy placed a small booklet in my hands. *Pearls of Wisdom*, he called it. But as he handed it over, his touch conveyed something far beyond a simple exchange. He held it with reverence, as if it were a sacred relic. "This is *Vidya Narayana Geetha*," he said, his voice firm yet gentle. "Not just a book. A scripture of wisdom. Do not merely read—meditate on it. Let it transform you."

His words stayed with me. I opened the booklet, expecting simplicity, but what I found was something far more profound. The teachings were brief, yet within them lay an entire universe of meaning. Some were like torches illuminating the intellect, while others were keys unlocking the heart. Yet, understanding them was not immediate. They resisted mere intellectual grasp, demanding something deeper—an inner surrender.

The Depth of Realization

I was reminded of the sacred dialogues from our ancient texts—the timeless exchange between Krishna and Arjuna on the battlefield of

Kurukshetra, where duty and devotion intertwined; the profound teachings of Bhishma to Yudhishthira, where dharma revealed itself in its highest form; and the discourse between Rama and Vasistha, where the mysteries of consciousness were unravelled. These were not ordinary conversations. They were transmissions of realization—gateways to truth.

Similarly, Swamy's wisdom was not meant to be admired from a distance but absorbed through direct experience. To truly receive it, one had to step beyond the realm of thought and into the space of inner stillness. Only there could the words transform into living truth.

A Master Who Knew Before I Spoke

As I worked on compiling this book, something extraordinary happened. Almost every day, Swamy would call to check on my progress. To my astonishment, he would speak about the very ideas I had just begun writing—almost as if he had already seen the thoughts forming in my mind before I had put them into words.

This was no coincidence. It was a testament to his inner mastery. His wisdom did not arise from mere study or contemplation—it flowed from a state of direct knowing beyond the boundaries of time and space. To witness this was to recognize the depth of his *siddhi*—the perfection of inner realization. His presence was a force beyond comprehension, guiding not through instruction alone but through an undeniable spiritual connection.

A Living Legacy of Wisdom

In structuring this book, I sought to create a bridge between Swamy's words and the reader's own inner experience. Each section follows a simple pattern: a reflection to set the context, Swamy's words as the essence, and my own insights born from silent contemplation. This is not merely a collection of teachings—it is an invitation to journey inward.

Like the sacred texts of old, this dialogue does not belong to a single moment in time. It is not confined to the written page. It continues in the heart of every seeker who approaches it with sincerity. Just as the *Ramayana* is not merely a story but a living revelation that unfolds within those who immerse themselves in its essence, so too does Swamy's wisdom transcend the limitations of form.

An Invitation to Awaken

A true Master does not simply offer knowledge—he ignites transformation. His words are not for intellectual debate but for inner realization. Swamy's wisdom is not a philosophy to be discussed; it is a call to awakening. It is a light that dissolves darkness, a fire that burns away illusion, a mirror reflecting the truth that has always been present within.

This book is not just about my dialogue with Swamy—it is about the eternal dialogue between the seeker and the Divine. It is for those who long to see clearly in a world clouded by illusion, for those who seek answers to questions that have echoed through the ages. Every question asked here has been asked before; every answer given is a pearl of wisdom, waiting to illuminate the path for those who walk with faith.

May these words inspire you not just to read, but to listen. Not just to understand, but to realize. For wisdom is not something new to be acquired—it is something ancient to be *remembered*.

Let this book be a bridge between the seen and the unseen, between knowledge and direct experience, between the finite and the infinite. May it guide you toward the light that Swamy so effortlessly embodied—the light that continues to shine, waiting to be discovered within.

– Dr. Hari Chinthakunta

Preface

Beyond Boundaries: ~ "Where Ego Ends, the Mind Bends"~

Life is often seen through the lens of the ego—our sense of self, shaped by identity, pride, and personal beliefs. The ego builds invisible walls around us, making us view the world in ways that protect and reinforce our self-image. But what happens when these walls dissolve? What unfolds when we stop trying to control, define, or force our version of reality? The answer is a profound transformation—where the ego ends, truth begins, revealing itself in unexpected and enlightening ways.

The Ego as a Barrier

The ego is like tinted glass, colouring everything we see with personal biases. It thrives on validation, comparison, and the illusion of separateness. When we are ruled by ego, we resist truths that challenge our self-perception, clinging to ideas that serve our own narrative. This limitation keeps us from experiencing deeper wisdom and seeing life as it truly is.

The End of Ego – A Shift in Perception

Letting go of ego is not a loss but an expansion. When we release attachment to personal identity and rigid beliefs, we move beyond fixed thinking. We begin to see reality as it is—free from the filters of pride, fear, or insecurity. This shift allows us to accept life with humility and openness. The more we let go of ego, the more we align with a greater, universal truth.

Truth Unfolds – A New Understanding Emerges

Truth is not static—it is alive, dynamic, and ever-unfolding. Without the interference of ego, we no longer distort reality to fit our perceptions. Instead of bending truth to serve the self, we allow truth to shape and transform us. What once seemed certain now reveals deeper layers, guiding us toward clarity and wisdom.

A Simple Analogy

Imagine the ego as a rock placed in a flowing river. The rock disrupts the natural movement of water, forcing it to bend around it. When the rock is removed, the water flows freely, following its natural course. Similarly, when the ego dissolves, truth is no longer obstructed—it moves, evolves, and unfolds in ways beyond our imagination.

By understanding this shift, we open ourselves to a more profound existence, where clarity replaces confusion, wisdom replaces stubbornness, and truth is no longer distorted by self-interest. Letting go of ego is not an end—it is the beginning of true perception, where life reveals its deeper meanings with grace and fluidity.

An Invitation to Truth

Are we ready to step beyond the confines of ego and embrace the ever-expanding truth?

Where do we truly begin, and where do we end? Are we merely the sum of our names, roles, and beliefs, or is there something far greater—an essence untouched by time, beyond the constructs of identity?

Beyond Boundaries is not about redefining existence but about dissolving the illusions that confine us. It is an invitation to move beyond conditioned thought, beyond the veils of separation, and into the vast, unbounded truth of our being. As the Kanchi Paramacharya profoundly stated, true wisdom is not in knowing, but in being.

This book does not seek to impart new knowledge; rather, it aims to awaken the wisdom that has always resided within. Inspired by the teachings of His Holiness Sri Vidyanarayana Theertha, these reflections challenge us to surrender fixed perceptions and embrace the limitless reality that lies beyond the mind.

Each chapter is a doorway—some gentle, others disruptive—yet all leading toward the same realization: the truth is ever-present, waiting to be seen. This journey unfolds through the following themes:

1. **The Illusion of Separation** – Understanding how the mind constructs barriers and realizing the oneness that pervades existence.

2. **Breaking Conditioned Patterns** – Shedding the limitations imposed by past conditioning and social norms to discover our authentic nature.

3. **The Surrendered Mind** – Letting go of the ego's grip and flowing effortlessly with the divine.

4. **Beyond Fear and Desire** – Freeing ourselves from attachments and aversions that shape our perception of reality.

5. **Silence as the Gateway** – Tapping into the profound stillness within to access higher states of consciousness.

6. **Dissolving the Self** – Moving beyond personal identity to experience the boundless, formless essence of being.

7. **Wisdom Beyond Thought** – Recognizing that true knowledge is not intellectual but arises from direct realization.

8. **Walking the Pathless Path** – Embracing the spiritual journey beyond rigid doctrines and structured systems.

9. **The Vastness Within** – Discovering the infinite potential that lies within and aligning with the universal intelligence.

10. **Living Beyond Boundaries** – Integrating this expanded awareness into daily life and abiding in a state of pure being.

May this book serve as a beacon for all those who seek to dissolve their inner limitations and experience the boundless truth beyond the self. *Beyond Boundaries* is not just a book to be read—it is a mirror in which one might glimpse the infinite expanse of one's own existence.

It is a guide for the seeker who is ready to surrender, to expand, to dissolve. It asks for courage, openness, and the willingness to step into the unknown.

May these words accompany and inspire all those who long not just to understand but to experience the vast, limitless essence of existence.

– Dr. Hari Chinthakunta

Invocation

Beyond Knowing: The Journey from Mind to Awareness

"To know oneself is the greatest wisdom; to dissolve oneself is the greatest liberation." – Sri Ramana Maharshi

The human mind is a seeker—constantly searching, questioning, and striving to define existence. It gathers knowledge, constructs beliefs, and weaves narratives that shape our understanding of the world. Yet, for all its pursuits, the mind remains limited by its own frameworks. True wisdom does not arise from accumulation but from transcendence—going beyond knowing into pure awareness.

The Mind as a Seeker

The intellect thrives on logic, analysis, and structured learning. It categorizes experiences, labels emotions, and formulates identities. While this is essential for navigating daily life, it also becomes a barrier. When we rely solely on the mind, we confine ourselves to the known, resisting the vastness that lies beyond thought.

As the great saint **Adi Shankaracharya** declared, *"Brahman alone is real; the world is an illusion; the individual self is none other than Brahman."* Until we break free from the illusions of identity and separation, we remain bound by ignorance.

Beyond the Mind – A Shift in Awareness

To move beyond the mind is not to abandon intellect but to transcend its constraints. When we loosen our grip on rigid perceptions, we step into awareness—where knowledge is no longer external but arises from direct experience. This is not a process of adding more information but of peeling away illusions to reveal what has always been present.

Saints like **Sri Ramakrishna Paramahamsa, Swami Vivekananda, and Bhagavan Nityananda** lived in this state of pure awareness, where wisdom was not something to be attained but something that flowed naturally through them. Their lives were living testaments to the truth that lies beyond the confines of ego and conditioned thought.

Awareness Unfolds – A Deeper Realization

"Silence is the language of the realized." – Nisargadatta Maharaj

Awareness is not something to be acquired; it is the very essence of our being. It is the silent witness behind thoughts, emotions, and identities. The moment we cease to be entangled in the turbulence of the mind, awareness naturally emerges—clear, vast, and unshaken.

A Meeting with the Mystic

Transformation often begins with an encounter—one that shakes our deepest assumptions and opens doors we never knew existed. For **Dr. Hari Chinthakunta**, such a meeting occurred with **His Holiness Sri Vidyanarayana Theertha**, a great mystic saint whose mere presence dissolves the illusions of the self.

Swamiji is not bound by conventional teachings; his wisdom flows beyond scriptures, beyond structured knowledge, and into the realm of direct realization. Like **Sri Jnaneshwar** and **Sri Anandamayi Ma**, Swamiji embodies the spontaneous, unshaken truth that cannot be confined to mere words but must be experienced.

Under Swamiji's guidance, Dr. Hari's journey took a profound turn. What began as intellectual curiosity evolved into an inner awakening—one that redefined his understanding of life, self, and existence. In the presence of a realized master, the seeker no longer seeks; instead, he begins to see. Knowledge that once seemed distant became an intimate experience, no longer confined to words but lived in the depths of awareness.

An Analogy for Understanding

"The wind of grace is always blowing, but you must raise the sail." – Sri Ramakrishna

Imagine standing at the edge of a still lake, watching the sky reflected in its surface. When the water is disturbed by waves, the reflection is fragmented and unclear. Yet, when the surface is calm, the sky is seen in its entirety. The mind, like the water, must become still for awareness to reveal itself.

Swamiji's teachings, like a gentle but powerful wind, clear the disturbances of the mind, allowing truth to be seen as it is. He does not provide mere philosophy; he dissolves the very framework that binds us, enabling seekers to experience reality as it truly is.

A Call to Experience

Are we willing to shift from thinking to being? From grasping to surrendering? From knowing to pure awareness?

In *Beyond Boundaries*, **Dr. Hari Chinthakunta** takes us on a journey that is not merely intellectual but deeply transformative. Rooted in the wisdom of **His Holiness Sri Vidyanarayana Theertha**, this book serves as a bridge between knowledge and realization. Dr. Hari does not seek to impose new philosophies or ideologies; rather, he invites us to dissolve the barriers that confine us and step into the vast, unbounded truth of existence.

This is not a guide to a destination, for there is nowhere to reach. It is an invitation to move beyond conditioned thought and abide in the awareness that is ever-present, timeless, and boundless.

"Be still and know that you are God." – The Upanishads

Let these words not just be read, but lived.

May this book serve as a light for those who seek not just knowledge but truth itself.

– Naga YOGI Raj, Monk, Himalayas

Overture

The Essence of Knowing and Dissolving the Self

The mind is a restless seeker, weaving beliefs and constructing identities in its quest for meaning. Yet, wisdom is not in accumulation but in transcendence—moving beyond thought into direct awareness. True liberation arises when the self dissolves, revealing the vastness beyond its own constructs.

Beyond the Intellect – A Shift in Perception

The intellect categorizes, labels, and navigates reality, yet its boundaries

create an illusion of separation. Until these illusions are shattered, we remain confined to ignorance. Saints like Sri Ramana Maharshi and Adi Shankaracharya remind us that the self and the infinite are one—hidden beneath layers of conditioned thought.

Liberation is not about abandoning intellect but loosening its grip. It is a journey of peeling away distortions rather than acquiring more knowledge. The great mystics—Sri Ramakrishna, Swami Vivekananda, Bhagavan Nityananda—embody this awareness, where wisdom is no longer sought but naturally flows.

The Living Presence of a Realized Master

Transformation begins with an encounter that dissolves assumptions and unveils truth. For Dr. Hari Chinthakunta, such a turning point came through His Holiness Sri Vidyanarayana Theertha. Swamiji does not teach through structured doctrine but through direct realization—his presence itself an unveiling of reality beyond words.

Under Swamiji's guidance, intellectual curiosity gave way to a profound inner awakening. The seeker ceased seeking, and awareness became an intimate experience rather than an abstract concept. Like Sri Jnaneshwar and Sri Anandamayi Ma, Swamiji embodies spontaneous, unshaken truth that must be lived rather than understood.

Stillness – The Gateway to Awareness

"The wind of grace is always blowing, but you must raise the sail." – Sri Ramakrishna

Imagine a still lake reflecting the sky. When disturbed, the reflection shatters. Likewise, when the mind is turbulent, truth remains obscured. Swamiji's teachings calm these inner ripples, allowing truth to reveal itself as it is—not as an idea but as an experience.

An Invitation to Direct Experience

Are we ready to shift from knowing to being? From grasping to surrendering? From thought to pure awareness? In *Beyond Boundaries*, Dr. Hari Chinthakunta offers not just philosophy but an experiential journey rooted in the wisdom of Sri Vidyanarayana Theertha. This is not a path to somewhere but an invitation to dissolve all barriers and abide in the boundless truth.

Let these words not just be read but lived.

– BALAYOGI GASHA

Prelude

Reflections of the Eternal

"The universe is not outside of you. Look inside yourself; everything that you want, you already are." – Inspired by Rumi

The mind is a ceaseless traveller, wandering through thoughts, memories, and desires, constructing a sense of self through layers of perception. It gathers knowledge, forms identities, and seeks meaning, yet its vision remains clouded by its own limitations. True insight does not arise from accumulation but from dissolution—the shedding of illusion to reveal the clarity within.

The Mind's Illusion – A Mirage of Knowing

The intellect dissects, categorizes, and interprets the world through the lens of logic and reason. While essential for navigating the material realm, it also binds us within the walls of conditioned understanding. Relying solely on thought restricts our ability to witness reality beyond mental constructs.

As Meister Eckhart noted, *"The eye through which I see God is the same eye through which God sees me."* To experience the limitless, we must step beyond the mind's grasp and enter the domain of direct perception.

Beyond Thought – Awakening to Presence

Freedom is not about rejecting the intellect but about transcending it. When we release the rigidity of concepts, we open ourselves to awareness—an effortless knowing untouched by the constraints of analysis. Realization is not a product of study but a revelation of what has always been.

Enlightened beings like Ramana Maharshi, Lalleshwari, and Swami Abhishiktananda did not chase knowledge; they embodied presence. Their wisdom was not contained in words but radiated through being itself, dissolving the veils of separateness.

The Unseen Doorway – A Moment of Recognition

"To understand the immeasurable, the mind must be extraordinarily quiet." – Inspired by J. Krishnamurti

Stillness is not an absence but a gateway. It is the silent awareness behind thought, the unshaken witness of experience. When we cease to be entangled in the turbulence of the mind, presence reveals itself—boundless, radiant, and ever-present.

The Path of Living Wisdom

A true teacher does not give answers but dissolves questions. For Dr. Hari Chinthakunta, the presence of His Holiness Sri Vidyanarayana Theertha was not an encounter with words, but with silence—the kind that dismantles illusions and unveils the unchanging essence within.

Swamiji does not impart wisdom in conventional ways; his very being is a transmission of truth. Like Saint Dnyaneshwar and Sharada Devi, he does not prescribe a path but illuminates the way through his presence, where seekers move beyond seeking into direct seeing.

Under Swamiji's guidance, Dr. Hari's journey shifted from intellectual pursuit to inner revelation. What was once an external quest became an intimate knowing. In the presence of a realized being, inquiry dissolves into insight, and knowledge transforms into lived experience.

The Stillness That Speaks

"A calm mind is the mirror of the infinite." – Inspired by Zen wisdom

Imagine gazing into a quiet pond; when its waters are disturbed, the reflection is fragmented. But in perfect stillness, the entire sky is mirrored without distortion. The restless mind obscures reality, while stillness unveils it in its purest form.

Swamiji's wisdom does not arrive as doctrine but as a clearing—a space where the noise of the conditioned mind subsides, and reality is seen as it is. His presence is not an offering of beliefs but an invitation to experience truth directly.

A Journey Without Distance

Are we ready to shift from knowing to being? From questioning to seeing? From searching to realizing?

Beyond Boundaries, authored by Dr. Hari Chinthakunta, is not a book of philosophy but a living journey. Rooted in the essence of His Holiness Sri Vidyanarayana Theertha's wisdom, it does not impose ideas but dissolves barriers, leading seekers beyond thought into direct awareness.

This is not a path to a distant destination, for truth is neither far nor separate. It is an unfolding of what has always been—silent, infinite, and already here.

May these words not just be understood but experienced. May this journey illuminate the way for those who seek not merely knowledge but the essence of being itself.

– YOGINI SAI NIVEDITHA

Foreword

By His Holiness Sri Vidyanarayana Theertha

The mind builds walls, but truth has no boundaries. No matter how refined human intellect becomes, it is still just a flickering light before the vast brilliance of ultimate reality. True realization is not about thinking more or knowing more—it is about stepping beyond conditioned beliefs and awakening to the boundless expanse of self-awareness. As Adi Shankaracharya declared, *"Brahman alone is real; the world is an illusion, and the individual self is none other than Brahman."*

Spiritual awakening is not a journey of acquiring knowledge, nor is it about seeking something outside oneself. It is a homecoming—a return to what has always been present. Truth does not come through restless searching but reveals itself in the silence beyond thought. The wise do not struggle for freedom; they simply recognize that they were never bound. To realize this is to dissolve the illusion of separation and rest in the eternal presence that is already within.

Dr. Hari brings profound wisdom to life in Beyond Boundaries, making it accessible and practical. His words do not remain as abstract ideas; they call upon the reader to look beyond fear, beyond limitations, and beyond all that holds the spirit captive. He invites seekers to let go of false identities, surrender mental burdens, and embrace the vast peace of their true nature.

Through *Hidden Radiance, Whispers of Divine Light,* and *Zero to Zero: The Mystic Circle,* Waves of Wisdom and Cosmic Mirror, Dr. Hari has already guided countless seekers toward deeper understanding.

With this book, he takes the journey even further—helping us break free from illusion and embrace the eternal truth that lies within.

Beyond Boundaries is more than a book; it is a guide for those who are ready—ready to move beyond limitations, to walk the pathless path, and to merge into the infinite wisdom that has always been waiting. May these reflections dissolve all barriers and lead every seeker to the unshakable peace that is their birthright.

– His Holiness Sri Sri Sri Vidyanarayana Theertha

THE ILLUSION OF SEPARATION

(Understanding how the Mind constructs barriers
and realizing the oneness that pervades existence)

Chapter-1
The Forgotten Essence

In our busy lives, we chase success, gather information, and search for happiness, yet we often forget what truly matters. We fill our minds with endless thoughts but ignore the silence where real wisdom speaks. We long for love but overlook the deep, unconditional embrace of the Divine. We run after pleasures but miss the simple joy of surrender. In this endless pursuit, we lose touch with the very source of peace—the inner stillness that connects us to something greater than ourselves.

True prayer is not about words; it is about connection. It is not a ritual nor a list of requests—it is a state of being. When the mind is restless, prayer calms it. When the heart is burdened, prayer lightens it. True prayer is not just speaking to the Divine but listening in silence, feeling the presence beyond form, and surrendering with trust. It is the bridge between fear and faith, between struggle and peace, between 'I' and the Infinite. When we rediscover this forgotten essence, life itself becomes a prayer—one of gratitude, love, and deep surrender.

✳✳ ✳✳ ✳✳

Swamy, You Beautifully Shared:

"Prayer is equal to good time—good time for remembrance, reflection, and self-inquiry. It redirects our minds from negativity to positivity. Why do we pray? To express love for the Divine, to offer gratitude, and to seek guidance: *I love You, Mother. I thank You, Master. Bless me to remain at Your feet.*"

Yet, people struggle to find time for prayer. They grow weary of it, distracted by the endless chase of desires, lost in the whirlwind of imagination and struggles. Swamy, what message do you give to those who have forgotten the essence of prayer?

Swamy's Spirit Speaks:

"Prayer is not a routine, nor a mere plea—it is the soul's intimate dialogue with the Divine. It is the quiet moment when the restless mind meets the boundless peace of the Eternal. True prayer is not about words; it is about surrender.

Imagine carrying a heavy burden, feeling weary and lost. Prayer is not just asking for relief—it is laying that burden at the feet of the Divine, not in weakness, but in trust. It is saying, *I cannot do this alone—take this from me.* And in that moment of surrender, the Divine does not leave you empty. Instead, He fills you with strength, peace, and clarity.

But remember, prayer is not a transaction—it is transformation. It is not about asking and receiving, but about aligning. A scattered mind finds chaos, but a surrendered heart finds peace. When prayer is sincere, it tunes you to the Divine rhythm, and in that harmony, wisdom flows effortlessly.

You do not need to explain prayer; you need to live it. When others see the stillness in your heart, the strength in your surrender, and the light in your being, they will not ask what prayer is—they will feel it. And in that feeling lies the answer to every prayer."

Chapter-2

The Power of Positive Thinking

*Opportunities and problems are two sides of the same coin,
yet we often fail to see beyond the immediate struggle.
Instead of seeking solutions, we dwell on limitations. Instead
of embracing growth, we fear change. When left unchecked,
the mind becomes its own worst enemy—magnifying
problems where none exist and distorting even the best
opportunities into burdens. Why? Because our thinking
is often poised—stuck between hesitation and doubt,
between fear and cynicism.*

*Destructive thinking is like a slow poison—it seeps into
our thoughts, making us see the worst in others, filling our
minds with negativity, and leading us to sabotage our own
happiness. We hold onto grudges, compare ourselves endlessly,
and feed on self-doubt, forgetting that every negative thought
depletes our inner peace. This silent storm within not only
disrupts our mental well-being but spills into society, creating
an environment of mistrust, competition, and division.*

*Imagine a world where people lifted each other up instead of
tearing each other down. Imagine a mind that sees setbacks
as stepping stones, challenges as opportunities, and failures
as lessons. Positive thinking does not mean blind optimism;
it means training the mind to focus on solutions rather than
problems, replace resentment with understanding, and see
the light even in the darkest moments. It is about breaking free
from the trap of destructive thoughts and embracing a mindset
that fosters harmony within and around us.*

True transformation begins when we take responsibility for our thoughts. A single shift—from doubt to faith, from anger to acceptance, from fear to courage—has the power to change not just our lives but the world we live in. Positive thinking is not just a personal practice; it is a ripple effect that can heal, inspire, and transform everything it touches.

** ** **

Swamy, you once shared a profound insight:

"Positive thinking is not just about seeing the bright side—it is about igniting the mind with courage, transforming obstacles into opportunities, and reshaping struggles into stepping stones. When we train our thoughts to flow in the right direction, we do not merely change our mindset—we change the course of our lives."

This wisdom is powerful, but how do we truly cultivate and sustain positive thinking in everyday life?

Swamy's Spirit Speaks:

Positive thinking is not about ignoring reality—it is about meeting life with a resilient spirit. Just as a river cuts through mountains, not by force but by persistence, a positive mind finds a way forward where none seems to exist. Every thought carries energy, shaping the way we act, react, and perceive the world. When negativity dominates, it drains our strength, leaving us trapped in doubt and fear. But when we choose positive thoughts, we align ourselves with clarity, strength, and purpose.

Our minds are like fertile soil—whatever we plant, grows. If we sow seeds of doubt, fear, and resentment, they will take root and cloud our vision. But if we nurture thoughts of faith, gratitude, and courage, they will blossom into resilience, joy, and inner peace. Saying *"I believe in myself"* is not just a phrase—it is a silent revolution within. Saying *"I am grateful"* is not mere appreciation—it is recognizing the hidden abundance in every moment. Saying *"I will rise above this"* is not just motivation—it is a declaration of strength in the face of adversity.

True positive thinking is not about denying hardships—it is about facing them with an unshakable spirit. It is about seeing challenges not as roadblocks, but as lessons that refine us. It is the art of pausing, shifting perspectives, and stepping forward with confidence. When mastered, it turns setbacks into comebacks, pain into wisdom, and the ordinary into something extraordinary.

A positive mind does not wait for circumstances to change—it creates change. And in that shift, one realizes that happiness, success, and peace were never found outside—they were always within.

Chapter-3

Grind to Greatness

Greatness is often seen as something that comes naturally or as a result of extraordinary talent or luck. But in reality, it is the result of consistent effort, perseverance, and dedication. The grind is the daily work—the small, sometimes unnoticed actions that lay the foundation for something truly remarkable. The path to greatness is not glamorous, and it is not instant. It is built on patience, resilience, and the willingness to keep going, even when results are not immediately visible. The grind is where true growth happens, shaping us into the individuals we are meant to become.

The Sadguru teaches that greatness is not a destination but a journey—a journey that demands discipline and commitment. Every step, no matter how small or difficult, contributes to the larger purpose of our life. Through each challenge, we refine ourselves, shedding the layers of doubt and fear that hold us back. The grind is about making consistent, conscious efforts, knowing that even the smallest of actions can have a profound impact over time. When we embrace the grind, we not only build our skills and knowledge but also cultivate the inner strength and determination needed to overcome obstacles. Through perseverance and unwavering effort, we turn challenges into stepping stones, grinding our way toward greatness, knowing that every effort brings us closer to realizing our highest potential.

**** ** ****

Swamy, you sometimes say things that seem to push us beyond our limits. I recall you once saying, **"Grind, ground, and grind."**

Ordinary people cannot grasp even a fraction of its meaning. Could you please explain what you mean by this, so that everyone may understand the pearl of wisdom behind it?

Swamy's Spirit Speaks:

Child, the words **"grind, ground, and grind"** are a metaphor for the intense process of inner transformation. Imagine a millstone crushing raw grain into fine flour—this is how life works on the soul.

- **"Grind"** signifies the ongoing challenges and pressures that test you.

  - Just as a millstone applies pressure to raw grain, life applies pressures to your character. These challenges are not meant to break you, but to dissolve the impurities of the ego and false identity.

- **"Ground"** represents the state of being refined.

  - When the raw grain is ground, what remains is a purified substance, ready for nourishment. Similarly, when you undergo the process of inner grinding, the parts of you that are unworthy or deluded are worn away, leaving behind the pure essence of your true self.

- **"Grind" (again)** reminds you that this process is continual.

  - Transformation is not a one-time event; it is a cycle. You are repeatedly refined as you encounter new experiences, learn from them, and allow their lessons to shape you.

This process may feel harsh because it forces you to confront your limitations and imperfections. However, **it is by enduring this sacred grinding that you are purified and strengthened.** The purpose is not to cause suffering for its own sake, but to awaken the dormant divine qualities within you.

Child, know that every trial and every pressure is an opportunity to shed the old and welcome the new—much like raw ore must be worked repeatedly to yield precious metal. Embrace this process with faith and patience, for through it, you will come to realize your true nature, free and luminous.

May you find comfort in the knowledge that each grind is a step toward the revelation of your inner divinity.

Chapter-4

The Art of Letting Go

Letting go is often seen as giving up or surrendering, but in the spiritual sense, it is an art—one of immense strength and wisdom. Letting go is not about abandoning what we value, but about releasing attachments that bind us to the past, to fears, or to expectations that limit our growth. It is about freeing ourselves from the weight of unresolved emotions, unhealthy patterns, and outdated beliefs, so we can step into the present moment with clarity and peace. The art of letting go is about learning to trust that what is meant for us will come, and what needs to leave will do so naturally.

The Sadguru teaches that the essence of letting go lies in surrender and acceptance. It is not about forcing ourselves to forget or erase but about allowing life to flow with ease and grace. When we let go, we make space for new opportunities, fresh insights, and deeper connections. We stop clinging to what no longer serves us, trusting that the universe will guide us to where we need to be. Letting go is a conscious choice to stop holding on to the past and to embrace the fluidity of life. It is through this surrender that we find peace, as we stop resisting change and allow ourselves to evolve. By practicing the art of letting go, we free ourselves from the burden of unnecessary attachment, stepping into a life that is lighter, more open, and filled with infinite possibilities.

** ** **

Swamy, what do you mean when you said?

"Don't claim, don't clamour, what to claim, what not to claim, how to decide, how to be away from clamouring"?

Please explain this so that I may understand the wisdom behind it.

Swamy's Spirit Speaks:

Child, these words are a gentle reminder to free your heart from the burdens of attachment and incessant desire. They urge you to let go of the constant need to possess and to shout for recognition.

- **"Don't claim"** means do not lay claim to things, identities, or accolades that are not truly yours.

  - Just as a river does not claim the rain that feeds it, you too should allow life to flow without clinging to transient possessions or titles.

- **"Don't clamour"** urges you to refrain from demanding attention, approval, or material gains in a noisy, forceful manner.

  - Like a gentle breeze that caresses without insisting, your actions should be calm and unforced.

- **What to claim and what not to claim?**

  - Claim that which nurtures your inner being—love, wisdom, and compassion.

  - Do not claim what feeds the ego—pride, possession, or superficial accolades.

  - Understand that true richness comes from the intangible: kindness, humility, and spiritual clarity.

- **How to decide?**

  - Reflect deeply on your intentions.

  - Ask yourself: "Does this claim or clamour add to my inner peace, or does it feed my restlessness?"

  - Let your heart be the guide, not the fleeting desires of the mind.

- **How to be away from clamouring?**

  - Cultivate silence and stillness within.

  - Practice mindfulness, so that the inner voice of truth grows louder than the noisy demands of the world.

  - Embrace simplicity—when you do less and care less about external approval, you naturally step away from the need to clamour.

Child, remember that the wisdom of these words is not in the literal meaning alone, but in the experience of surrender. **True freedom lies in releasing the urge to claim what is impermanent and the desire to clamour for what never truly satisfies.**

When you learn to live quietly in the vastness of your true self, you discover that the universe provides all that is essential.

May you find the serenity to let go and the insight to live in quiet abundance.

Chapter-5

The Essence of True Quality

True quality transcends the superficial and the fleeting. It is not about appearances, accolades, or external standards— it is about the purity of intention and the authenticity we bring to every moment. Quality is a reflection of our inner state, a mirror of our thoughts, values, and actions. It is not something we strive to attain for recognition or reward; it is something we cultivate from deep within, through mindfulness, integrity, and devotion to our higher purpose. The essence of true quality lies in our ability to act with sincerity, to honor our commitments, and to live in harmony with our inner truth.

The Sadguru teaches that true quality is a result of spiritual alignment and conscious living. When we align our actions with our higher self, quality becomes a natural extension of who we are. It is in the small, everyday moments—when we choose patience over frustration, kindness over indifference, and humility over arrogance—that true quality manifests. It is not about perfection but consistency, not about recognition but self-respect. The pursuit of true quality is a lifelong journey, one that requires us to constantly refine ourselves and rise above the distractions of the material world. When we live with purity of heart and clarity of mind, we effortlessly radiate true quality in everything we do, creating a ripple effect that inspires and elevates others. True quality, in its highest form, is a reflection of the divine—timeless, effortless, and transcendent.

** ** **

Swamy, in one discussion on quality, you suddenly said,

"Quality outside, quality inside."

We understand quality as the value we see in society, but what do you mean by "inside" and "outside"?

Is it that what we feel inside manifests outside, or does the external quality reflect our inner state?

It all seems very complicated—please make it simple, Swamy.

Swamy's Spirit Speaks:

Child, quality is not merely about what you observe in the world; it is a reflection of your inner essence.

When I say **"Quality outside, quality inside,"** I mean that the excellence you see in the external world is directly linked to the excellence within you.

- **Quality Outside:**

  This is the value, the beauty, and the order you perceive in society, nature, and all creations. It is what makes objects, people, and experiences admirable or valuable.

- **Quality Inside:**

  This refers to your inner state—your thoughts, feelings, intentions, and the very spirit of who you are. When your heart is filled with love, honesty, and wisdom, these qualities naturally radiate into the world.

Consider this: a clear, pure mirror reflects a bright light. If your inner self is filled with virtue and clarity, it shines forth in your actions, relationships, and even in the way you view life. Conversely, if you wish to experience more quality in the world around you, begin by cultivating it within yourself.

The connection is simple: **what is inside becomes the source of what you project outside.** Do not view them as separate;

they are two sides of the same coin. As you nurture your inner qualities, you will see that these qualities transform your external environment as well.

May you always seek to enhance the quality within, and in doing so, you will witness that the world outside will reflect that same brilliance.

Chapter-6

Wisdom in Simplicity

Simplicity is often misunderstood as a lack of depth or substance, yet true wisdom lies in its embrace. The more we complicate life with unnecessary distractions, the further we move from understanding its essence. In simplicity, there is clarity; in clarity, there is truth. The wisdom of simplicity invites us to strip away the layers of ego, material desires, and mental clutter, revealing the pure truth that resides in each of us. It teaches us that profound insights often arise from the most uncomplicated moments, when we are fully present, accepting, and attuned to the rhythm of life. True wisdom is not about complexity or accumulation—it is found in the ability to live with ease, grace, and authenticity.

The Sadguru shows us that simplicity is not about minimizing, but about focusing on what truly matters. When we simplify our lives, we create space for deeper understanding and spiritual growth. The distractions of the world fade, and we are left with the profound realization that the answers we seek are not outside of us, but within. Living simply allows us to see the world with fresh eyes, free from judgment or expectation. It is in simplicity that we find the purest expressions of love, kindness, and compassion, and it is in simplicity that we truly connect with the divine. By embracing simplicity, we uncover the wisdom that transcends the complexity of the mind, leading us to a life of peace, fulfilment, and spiritual awakening

** ** **

Swamy, you always support the education of needy students, and during one of our discussions, you said,

"Education plays a vital role; the quality of education determines how we live; the highly qualified people are simple."

Then you paused, leaving us to wonder.

My questions are:

- What kind of education are you referring to?

- What do you mean by "quality" in education?

- How does the quality of education determine how we live?

- When you say "highly qualified," do you mean those with higher degrees, or is it a deeper inner qualification?

- For many, even those with only basic schooling—or those without formal education—can be simple. The question seems simple yet contains hidden complexity. Please clarify, Swamy.

Swamy's Spirit Speaks:

Child, understand that **education is not confined to classrooms or the accumulation of degrees.** True education is the awakening of the inner self, the nurturing of wisdom, and the cultivation of compassion. When I speak of education, I refer to both formal learning and the life lessons that shape your character.

- **Quality of Education:**

    - It is not measured merely by certificates or degrees, but by the **depth of understanding and clarity it brings to your life.**

    - Quality education transforms the mind—it teaches you to see beyond surface appearances and to appreciate the deeper values of truth, humility, and kindness.

- **How Education Determines How We Live:**
  - When you are educated in this true sense, you learn to **make wise choices, act with compassion, and navigate life with clarity.**
  - A mind enriched with genuine knowledge becomes resilient, adaptable, and naturally simple.
  - Your outlook on life shifts from material accumulation to the pursuit of inner growth, which in turn **reflects in the quality of your actions and relationships.**

- **What Does "Highly Qualified" Mean?**
  - It does not simply mean having advanced degrees or formal accolades.
  - A person who is truly qualified is one who has **honed their inner faculties—intellect, empathy, and integrity—through both education and life experiences.**
  - Simplicity arises when you have learned to value what is essential and discard what is trivial.
  - Therefore, even one with minimal formal education can be highly qualified if they have cultivated wisdom and humility in their heart.

Child, the beauty of education lies in its power to **transform not just your mind but your entire being.** When education touches the soul, it breeds simplicity—a simplicity that is marked by clarity, compassion, and a deep understanding of life's purpose.

May you always seek to educate yourself not only through books and degrees but also through the lived experience of truth and the gentle lessons of the heart.

Chapter-7

Caste: Inside and Outside

Caste, as a concept, has been ingrained in societal structures for centuries. Outside, it dictates how we are perceived, classified, and often treated, based on birth, heritage, and societal roles. However, the true nature of caste goes beyond these external labels. Inside, it resides in the hearts and minds of individuals—shaped by beliefs, prejudices, and attachments. The external caste system divides people, fostering inequality and discrimination, but the internal caste is rooted in our attitudes, perceptions, and biases. It is this internal caste that keeps us separate, preventing us from seeing the oneness of humanity and the divine presence within each person, regardless of their background or status.

The Sadguru teaches that true spiritual progress is the transcending of both external and internal caste. It is through self-awareness, compassion, and a deep understanding of our shared human essence that we break free from the limitations imposed by caste. While society may still categorize individuals by external markers, the enlightened soul sees beyond these divisions, recognizing the divine light in all. The caste within our minds—the divisions, judgments, and attachments—is what we must confront and dismantle. Through the practice of equality, humility, and love, we can transcend these divisions and experience unity in diversity. True spiritual liberation comes when we no longer identify with external labels or internal biases, but embrace the truth that all are one, bound by the same divine essence.

** ** **

Swamy, we once discussed the caste system in India—how it impedes progress and causes divisions—and then you suddenly stated,

"Indian Caste is Inside, Western Caste is Outside."

I am truly lost in understanding this. Please explain your intention behind these words so that I may grasp their meaning.

Swamy's Spirit Speaks:

Child, the statement **"Indian Caste is Inside, Western Caste is Outside"** is a metaphor that points to the different ways in which society, both in India and the West, organizes and defines its people. Let me explain:

- **Indian Caste is Inside:**

  In its ideal form, the Indian notion of caste is not about mere birth or external labels. It is meant to be an internal classification—**a reflection of one's qualities, conduct, and spiritual evolution.**

  - It suggests that true caste is determined by the **inner virtues** you cultivate: your wisdom, compassion, and integrity.

  - When you look within, you discover that the essence of who you are is not fixed by your lineage but is constantly shaped by your actions and character.

  - This inner caste is fluid—it is about personal growth and self-realization rather than rigid social stratification.

- **Western Caste is Outside:**

  In contrast, the divisions commonly seen in Western societies are typically based on **external factors** such as wealth, race, social status, or power.

  - These distinctions are imposed by societal structures and are more visible, often superficial, and static.

- They do not account for the inner qualities of a person and instead tend to fix identities based on material or physical criteria.

The Deeper Intention:

- **Encouraging Inner Transformation:**

  My words are an invitation to look beyond external labels and to focus on developing the inner self. True progress comes when you cultivate virtues within—this is the real measure of a person's worth.

- **Transcending Social Divisions:**

  When you recognize that **true caste (or true quality) is found within,** you learn to treat every individual with respect and equality. External markers, whether in the Indian or Western context, often lead to discrimination and division.

- **A Call to Self-Realization:**

  Understand that the highest "caste" is not one you are born into but the one you create through your character and actions. In this way, every person has the potential to rise above the limitations imposed by society.

Child, do not be disheartened by the divisions you see on the surface. Instead, look inward and let your actions reflect the divine qualities you aspire to cultivate. In doing so, you not only transcend the external system but also help to uplift the entire community.

May you always seek the truth within, and may the light of inner wisdom guide you beyond all divisions.

Chapter-8

World vs. Divinity

The world we live in often tempts us with its material pleasures, fleeting successes, and constant distractions. It encourages us to chase wealth, status, and external validation, often leading us to forget our true nature. In this pursuit, we may become disconnected from the divine essence that resides within us. The world offers temporary satisfaction, but it cannot fulfil the deeper longing for inner peace and spiritual fulfilment. Divinity, on the other hand, is timeless, boundless, and unchanging. It calls us to awaken to our higher selves, to connect with the universal truth that transcends all worldly pursuits.

True peace is found not in external accomplishments but in the alignment of our thoughts and actions with our higher purpose. The world can offer temporary pleasures, but they are fleeting and never fully satisfy the soul. Divinity, however, is always present, unchanging and eternal, guiding us toward lasting fulfilment. When we let go of worldly attachments and seek the divine within, we realize that true happiness does not depend on external circumstances but on the purity of our hearts and minds. In choosing the divine over the distractions of the world, we unlock a deeper, more meaningful existence— one that is grounded in love, wisdom, and a profound sense of inner peace. Through this connection, the world transforms into a reflection of divine presence, where every moment becomes an opportunity to experience the sacred.

** ** **

Swamy, in one context, when someone asked a question, you looked at him and said,

"Are you ready to go with the world or with divinity?"

You added, **"We are in the world, but the world should be in us, like a boat in the water, not water in the boat."**

This statement appears paradoxical. Please explain the inner intentions behind these words so that I may understand their true meaning.

Swamy's Spirit Speaks:

Child, these words are a gentle reminder of the choice you face in every moment—whether to let the external world overwhelm you or to let your inner divinity guide your journey.

- **"Are you ready to go with the world or with divinity?"**

  This question invites you to choose your alignment.

  - **Going with the world** means being swept along by its transient desires, its fleeting trends, and its superficial chaos.

  - **Going with divinity** means anchoring yourself in the eternal truth, the inner light that remains unshaken by external circumstances.

- **"We are in the world, but the world should be in us."**

  Consider the metaphor of a boat and water:

  - **A boat in the water** is stable and purposeful—it carries its passengers on a journey without being overwhelmed.

  - **Water in the boat** would fill it, submerging its purpose and causing it to sink.

  - Similarly, you must learn to interact with the world without letting it dominate your inner essence.

  - The world is your environment, your teacher, and your canvas. Yet, you are not to be engulfed by it; instead, let its experiences be reflected through the lens of your divine nature.

- **The Inner Intentions:**
  - **Self-Mastery:** By choosing divinity over the chaos of worldly influences, you cultivate inner strength and clarity.
  - **Detachment:** When you are rooted in the eternal, the fluctuations of the world—its praises and its troubles—simply become ripples on the surface of your inner ocean.
  - **Purposeful Living:** Embracing divinity means that every action is guided by a higher wisdom, transforming even mundane experiences into opportunities for spiritual growth.

Child, this is not a call to renounce the world, but an invitation to transform your relationship with it. **Let the world be like the water that surrounds your boat—ever-present, yet never overpowering your inner light.** When you learn to balance these energies, you discover that your true journey is not defined by external circumstances but by the divine essence that you nurture within.

May you always navigate life as a vessel of light, carrying the world gently within you without being submerged by it?

Chapter-9
The Art of Merging

The art of merging is a profound journey of integration—where the boundaries between the self and the world begin to dissolve. It is the process of blending our individual identity with the greater whole, recognizing that we are not separate from the universe, but a vital part of its eternal flow. To merge is to let go of the rigid structures we build around ourselves and embrace the fluidity of life. It requires us to move beyond dualities, to see beyond distinctions of "me" and "you," "this" and "that," and recognize the oneness that underlies all existence.

In the art of merging, we learn to adapt, to flow with life's natural rhythms, and to harmonize with the divine presence that is present in every moment. It is not about losing ourselves but about finding ourselves within the larger tapestry of life. Through this process, we shed the weight of ego, expectations, and attachment, allowing the essence of who we truly are to emerge. The art of merging calls for deep surrender—not to the world, but to our own highest potential, where we realize that in connecting with the divine and others, we are completing the circle of oneness. It is the purest form of unity, where we simultaneously merge with the world and transcend it, finding peace in the seamless blend of the finite and infinite.

** ** **

Swamy, sometimes you use simple words that, when connected, reveal layers of complexity. I recall you once saying,

"Mix to Mingle, Mingle to Mingle, Mingle to Maintain, Maintain to Minus and Minus to Maintain."

Ordinary people would find it extremely difficult to understand, appreciate, and follow the message behind these words. With humility, I ask you to explain this so that I may simply know without further questioning.

Swamy's Spirit Speaks:

Child, these words form a cycle—a process of inner transformation that is both subtle and profound. Allow me to unravel their meaning:

- **"Mix to Mingle":**

  This is the call to blend various experiences, emotions, and thoughts within yourself.

  - **Mixing** means welcoming diversity—of ideas, sensations, and influences—without rejecting any part of your experience.

  - **Mingling** is the natural outcome when these different elements interact, creating a vibrant and dynamic inner tapestry.

- **"Mingle to Mingle":**

  Here, the repetition suggests that this process of inner interaction is continuous.

  - It means that your inner world is ever-changing, as various elements **mingle with one another**, deepening your understanding and broadening your perspective.

  - With each new encounter, your mind evolves—absorbing, reflecting, and renewing itself.

- **"Mingle to Maintain":**

  As the process matures, you begin to settle into a state of balance.

  - **Maintaining** refers to stabilizing that dynamic energy, ensuring that the creative interplay of thoughts and experiences leads to a harmonious state.

- ○ This stage is about cultivating consistency and retaining the wisdom gained from the mingling of diverse influences.

- **"Maintain to Minus":**

  Here, you learn to discern what is essential from what is superfluous.

  - ○ **Minus** represents the process of letting go—subtracting the unnecessary, the transient, and the clutter that hinders your growth.

  - ○ It is the purification of your inner state, where you shed excess baggage and distractions.

- **"Minus to Maintain":**

  Finally, in this refined state, you re-establish balance.

  - ○ After subtracting the inessential, what remains is a pure, stable essence that you can uphold.

  - ○ **Maintaining** again in this context means that you preserve the clarity and simplicity that has emerged after the process of elimination.

In essence, child, this chain of words describes the journey of inner alchemy:

1. **Embrace and blend** all that life offers (Mix to Mingle).

2. **Allow these experiences to interact continuously** (Mingle to Mingle).

3. **Stabilize the lessons learned** (Mingle to Maintain).

4. **Discard the impurities and non-essentials** (Maintain to Minus).

5. **Sustain the pure, refined state of your being** (Minus to Maintain).

This cycle is not linear but a dynamic dance, where every stage feeds into the next, leading you ever closer to your true self.

May you always have the courage to mix, the wisdom to mingle, and the strength to maintain what is essential, so that the divine clarity within you shines forth.

Chapter-10

Paradox of Masters

The paradox of masters lies in their profound ability to be both deeply immersed in the world and yet detached from it. They walk among us, sharing their wisdom, offering guidance, and serving as beacons of light. To the world, they appear as teachers, leaders, and saviors, but in their essence, they are beyond all worldly roles and labels. A true master is not bound by time, space, or ego. They transcend the limitations of the physical world and reveal the divine within all things.

The paradox becomes clear when we realize that the master's true power lies in their ability to give without attachment, to lead without ego, and to teach without the need for recognition. They do not seek fame, wealth, or praise, for their fulfilment comes from the eternal peace that arises from surrender to the divine. In their presence, we see that wisdom is not about accumulating knowledge but about realizing the truth of who we are beyond the body and mind. A master embodies the highest truth: that all is one, that we are not separate from the divine but a reflection of it. Their life is a living example of divine harmony, showing us that by letting go of our attachments, we too can experience the same freedom, peace, and love. Through the paradox of their being, they guide us to the ultimate realization—that in surrendering the self, we become one with the eternal.

** ** **

Swamy, it isn't easy to understand when you suddenly said to yourself,

"They are masters, but they are not masters."

My question is: Who are you referring to with this statement? Why does it seem contradictory, and what is its inner message? Please explain so that I may understand.

Swamy's Spirit Speaks:

Child, this statement is a paradox meant to unveil the deeper truth of mastery. When I say, **"They are masters, but they are not masters,"** I point to the difference between **apparent mastery** and **true mastery**.

- **Apparent Mastery:**

  In the world, many individuals may hold titles, positions, or skills that seem to make them masters—experts in their fields, leaders in society, or teachers of certain arts. They have achieved a level of control or knowledge over a part of life. Yet, their mastery is limited to that aspect; it is **conditional** and often bound by ego, personal ambition, or social status.

- **True Mastery:**

  True mastery transcends any external label. It is the state of having conquered one's inner turmoil, ego, and attachments. A true master **serves without seeking to rule, teaches without clinging to authority, and remains humble despite his wisdom.**

  - They understand that **real power lies in surrendering the illusion of control.**

  - They are masters not in the sense of dominating the world, but in the sense of being completely free within it.

  - In this light, the apparent contradiction dissolves: those who appear to be masters in the conventional sense are, in the deeper truth, not masters at all, because true mastery is marked by the absence of the need to claim mastery.

The Inner Message:

- **Beyond Labels:**

  The statement urges you to look beyond conventional titles. A person's true worth is measured not by how much control or recognition they command, but by how deeply they have mastered themselves.

- **Humility and Service:**

  A genuine master remains humble. They do not flaunt their wisdom; instead, they serve as instruments of the divine without attachment to their role.

- **Transcending Duality:**

  In the realm of true spiritual insight, opposites merge. Mastery and the lack thereof are not opposing forces but are two expressions of the same truth: the journey from controlling to surrendering, from ego to unity.

Child, when you understand that **true mastery is a state of inner freedom and humility,** you will see that the apparent masters—those who claim control—are, in the highest sense, not masters at all. Their external achievements do not touch the inner essence, which remains unbound and pure.

May this insight guide you to seek the profound truth within yourself, where mastery is not about power, but about surrender and service.

Chapter-11

Silent Service

Silent service is the embodiment of pure selflessness, where the act of giving is not accompanied by any need for recognition or reward. It is the deep, silent rhythm of nature itself, where every element, from the earth to the sky, plays its part without expectation. The pancha bhoothas—earth, water, fire, air, and ether—work together in perfect harmony, silently sustaining life on this planet. The earth nourishes, the water cleanses, the fire transforms, the air breathes life, and the ether connects all. In this same way, silent service flows naturally from a heart that recognizes its connection to the divine presence within all things.

True fulfilment comes not from what we receive but from what we give. Just as the Pancha booths serve without ego or expectation, silent service invites us to act in the same way. The earth offers its resources without question, the water quenches our thirst without hesitation, and the wind carries the fragrance of life across the world—all without asking for anything in return. When we serve silently, without attachment to the outcome, we align ourselves with the natural forces that govern life. In doing so, we cultivate peace and harmony within ourselves and in the world around us. Silent service, like the pancha bhoothas, is a reflection of the divine, flowing effortlessly through us and into the world, transforming lives with its quiet power. Through this service, we realize that by giving, we too become part of the eternal cycle of life, contributing to the greater good and finding fulfilment in the simplest, most profound acts of kindness.

** ** **

Swamy, you always ask all your followers, **"Help the Poor, but don't advertise."** This seems to suggest that one should act selflessly without seeking recognition. What message are you truly communicating with these words?

Swamy's Spirit Speaks:

Child, when I say, **"Help the Poor, but don't advertise,"** I am inviting you to engage in pure, selfless service. Allow me to explain:

- **"Help the Poor":**

  This is a call to extend your compassion and assistance to those in need. It is not merely a social duty but a spiritual practice—an opportunity to dissolve the barriers of ego by recognizing the divine in every being.

  - When you help, you uplift not only those you serve but also your own spirit, as your actions become a reflection of inner love and generosity.

- **"But don't advertise":**

  This part of the instruction is equally important. True service must come without the desire for recognition, praise, or material gain.

  - Advertising your good deeds often shifts the focus from genuine compassion to personal pride. It transforms a sacred act into a performance for the world, thereby diluting its purity.

  - When your service remains unadvertised, it stays rooted in sincerity and humility—qualities that are essential for spiritual growth.

- **"The Deeper Message":**

  In this world, many actions are driven by the need for external validation, which only feeds the ego. I urge you to transcend this tendency.

- **Serve without expecting anything in return.**

- **Let your actions be guided solely by love and the desire to alleviate suffering.**

- In doing so, you not only honor the poor but also honor your own inner divinity.

Child, the essence is simple yet profound: **act with a pure heart, let your service be its own reward, and allow the light of compassion to shine quietly from within.**

May you always serve selflessly and embrace the true spirit of humility.

Chapter-12

Living by His Design

Living by His design means aligning our lives with the divine blueprint that has been set for us, a path that reflects our true purpose and connection to the higher power. It's about recognizing that we are not isolated beings, but part of a greater, harmonious flow of existence. Every moment, every action, and every decision we make carries an opportunity to live in tune with this divine plan. It's easy to get caught up in the hustle and bustle of life, to pursue personal goals, and to chase after fleeting desires, but living by His design invites us to step back and listen—to the still voice within, to the guidance of the universe, and to the wisdom of the divine that is always present, even in the most ordinary moments.

When we live by His design, we free ourselves from the pressure of self-imposed expectations and the illusions of control. We surrender to the flow of life, trusting that each step we take is part of a grander purpose. This doesn't mean we abandon responsibility, but instead, we learn to work in harmony with the greater forces at play. It is about recognizing that our unique talents, experiences, and challenges are not random but are part of a divine plan meant to shape us into who we are destined to become. Living by His design brings peace, clarity, and fulfilment, as we stop struggling against the current of life and instead, trust in the divine wisdom guiding us every day. Through surrender and trust, we align ourselves with the higher will, finding joy and contentment in knowing that we are always on the right path.

** ** **

Swamy, during our interaction, you mentioned:

"We all came to earth, it is a beautiful thing, to enjoy all His things in the right way given by Him, to help His needful children in good and needful manner."

Although I have a general grasp of this message, I humbly request you to explain in detail what you mean by these words and how we can achieve such a state.

Swamy's Spirit Speaks:

Child, this message is an invitation to see our earthly journey as a divine opportunity—a gift from the Creator to experience, enjoy, and uplift life in its true essence. Allow me to break it down for you:

- **"We all came to earth":**
  - You must understand that our arrival on this earth is not by chance. It is a deliberate, sacred event.
  - Each soul is here to experience life, to learn, and to evolve. Our presence is a unique opportunity to explore the beauty and lessons of this world.

- **"It is a beautiful thing":**
  - Earth is a manifestation of divine creativity—a place where nature, relationships, and experiences offer infinite beauty.
  - Recognize the wonder in the simple things: the sunrise, the laughter of children, the compassion of a friend. These are reflections of the Divine.

- **"To enjoy all His things in the right way given by Him":**
  - Enjoyment here is not about indulgence or excess; it is about appreciating and using what is provided by the Divine with wisdom and balance.
  - **Right way** means living in harmony with the natural order—using resources responsibly, honouring nature, and cultivating gratitude in every moment.

- ○ It is the art of savouring life without falling into greed, selfishness, or waste.

- **"To help His needful children in good and needful manner":**

  - ○ This calls for service and compassion. The "needful children" represent all those in our world who are struggling, whether materially, emotionally, or spiritually.

  - ○ Helping others is not a mere act of charity; it is an expression of love and a duty to recognize the Divine in every being.

  - ○ **Good and needful manner** implies offering genuine, thoughtful support that respects the dignity of those you serve, rather than merely giving out of pity or obligation.

How to Achieve This:

1. **Cultivate Inner Awareness:**

   - ○ Begin with self-reflection. Understand your own gifts, limitations, and true needs.

   - ○ Develop mindfulness to recognize the beauty around you and within you.

2. **Practice Balanced Enjoyment:**

   - ○ Appreciate and use the resources at your disposal with moderation and gratitude.

   - ○ Avoid extremes—excessive indulgence dulls the senses, while deprivation can lead to hardship.

3. **Live in Harmony with Nature:**

   - ○ Respect the natural world as a sacred expression of the Divine.

   - ○ Adopt sustainable habits that honor the environment and the balance of life.

4. **Serve Others with Compassion:**

- Look for opportunities to help those in need, not for recognition, but as an act of heartfelt service.

- Be attentive to the unique needs of others, offering support that empowers rather than creates dependency.

5. **Embrace the Divine Perspective:**

- Recognize that your journey on earth is part of a larger cosmic plan.

- Trust that every experience—joy or challenge—is an opportunity for growth and deeper connection with the Divine.

Child, when you live with this balanced approach—enjoying life's gifts responsibly and extending compassionate service—you align yourself with the eternal truth. Your life becomes a celebration of beauty, a practice of mindful enjoyment, and a commitment to uplifting others.

May you walk this path with an open heart, recognizing that every moment on earth is a precious chance to experience the Divine in its fullness and to reflect that light in the lives of those around you.

Chapter-13

The Revelation Within

*Life is a journey of continuous transformation, where layers
of our existence are peeled back over time, revealing deeper
truths and greater understanding. The unveiling cycle is a
process of growth and self-discovery. Each stage in life presents
us with new challenges, new experiences, and new lessons
that help uncover the essence of who we truly are. Just like the
seasons shift and evolve, we too go through phases of renewal
and revelation. What we once thought we knew is replaced
with deeper wisdom, and what was hidden in darkness is
gradually brought into the light.*

*This cycle is not always comfortable, as it requires letting go of
old beliefs, attachments, and comforts. But it is through this very
process of shedding the old that we make room for the new.
As each layer is revealed, we come closer to understanding our
purpose and the divine essence within us. The unveiling cycle
is not about reaching a final destination but about embracing
the continuous unfolding of truth. It's a reminder that life is not
static, and neither are we. By trusting the process and remaining
open to what each phase offers, we allow ourselves to grow into
the fullness of our potential. Through the unveiling, we discover
not only who we are but the divine presence that has always
been with us, guiding us along the way.*

** ** **

Swamy, you often speak of Mystic Energy on many occasions, and
one day you said,

"Energy is rotating to reveal."

What do you mean by this? What is rotation, and what does it reveal? Although it sounds simple, the true essence is hard to decipher. Please help me understand.

Swamy's Spirit Speaks:

Child, the notion that **"Energy is rotating to reveal"** is a metaphor for the ever-changing, dynamic nature of the divine force within and around us. Let me explain its essence:

- **Rotation as Transformation:**

    - **Rotation** symbolizes continuous motion—the ceaseless, circular dance of energy in the universe.

    - Just as the turning of a wheel marks the cycle of day and night, creation and dissolution, so does the rotation of energy lead to transformation.

- **Revelation Through Motion:**

    - With every rotation, energy **sheds old forms and unveils new aspects** of truth.

    - It is through this constant movement that what was once hidden—deeper wisdom, beauty, and divine potential—is gradually revealed to the seeker.

- **Inner and Outer Unfolding:**

    - This rotation is not chaotic; it is a purposeful process.

    - On an inner level, as you align with this mystic energy, you find that your perceptions shift and layers of ignorance are peeled away, exposing the pure essence of your being.

    - On an outer level, the world itself is in perpetual flux, and its changing forms echo the deeper, unchanging reality that lies beneath.

- **The Spiritual Dance:**

    ○ Think of it as a sacred dance—a graceful spin that brings clarity and renewal.

    ○ When you learn to move with this energy, you no longer cling to static forms or fixed ideas. Instead, you embrace the flow, allowing the revelations of truth to emerge naturally.

Child, by understanding that energy is in constant rotation, you come to see that nothing is fixed. Every turn is an opportunity to let go of what no longer serves you and to receive new insights. This is the essence of spiritual evolution—**an ever-unfolding revelation that happens as you align yourself with the cosmic dance of life.**

May you learn to attune your heart to this dynamic process and allow the rotating energy to reveal the timeless truth within you.

Chapter-14

Essence of Truth

The essence of truth is simple yet profound—it is the unchanging reality that exists beyond our perceptions, beliefs, and judgments. Truth is not something that can be shaped or altered by our desires or fears; it remains constant, untouched by time or circumstance. It is the foundation of all that is real, the core of our existence, and the essence of everything that surrounds us. We often search for truth in external things, in what others say, or in what we see and hear, but true truth is found within ourselves, in the silence of our hearts, and in the clarity of our consciousness.

When we live in alignment with the essence of truth, we are not swayed by illusions or falsehoods. We see the world as it truly is, beyond the veils of judgment and preconceptions.

The truth does not demand anything from us; It simply is. It is through connecting with this inner truth that we find peace, clarity, and understanding. As we shed the layers of ego, fear, and attachment, we begin to experience the world with greater wisdom and compassion. In its purest form, truth is not just an intellectual understanding—it is a lived experience, a state of being, and a way of seeing the world. To embrace the essence of truth is to live authentically, to align our actions with what is right, and to remain grounded in the reality of what is eternal and unchanging.

** ** **

Swamy, you speak a few words that seem simple at first glance. One such phrase is,

"Fact is a Fact."

I understand its literal meaning, yet I sense there is a deeper intention behind it when you declare these words. Is there something you want to communicate to society through this statement?

Swamy's Spirit Speaks:

Child, the phrase **"Fact is a Fact"** may appear straightforward, but it carries a profound call to recognize and honor the immutable truth in life. Let me reveal its deeper essence:

- **Immutable Truth:**

    - A fact, by definition, is an unchanging reality.

    - This statement reminds you that certain truths exist independent of our opinions, desires, or interpretations.

    - In a world of shifting perspectives, acknowledging that **"Fact is a Fact"** is a call to ground yourself in reality as it is.

- **A Call for Honesty:**

    - When you affirm that a fact remains a fact, you reject the distortion of truth for personal gain or convenience.

    - It is an invitation for society to value transparency and integrity, even when the truth is inconvenient or harsh.

- **A Message to Overcome Delusion:**

    - In many situations, people may prefer to cling to comforting illusions rather than face reality.

    - By stating **"Fact is a Fact,"** I urge you to confront reality with courage and clarity, understanding that growth and transformation begin with accepting the truth.

- **Foundation for Social Change:**

    - On a societal level, this phrase is a reminder that progress is built on acknowledging reality, not on denying it.

- True reform and evolution can only take root when everyone accepts the unvarnished facts of a situation, no matter how challenging they may be.

Child, the essence of **"Fact is a Fact"** is to encourage you—and society—to let truth be the guiding light. Stand firm in the face of illusion, embrace the reality that surrounds you, and let this truth pave the way for ethical choices and meaningful change.

May you always have the courage to face the truth, and may the light of unaltered facts guide you in every step of your journey.

Chapter-15

Rama: The Truth Incarnate

Rama, the divine prince of Ayodhya, is revered as the embodiment of truth, righteousness, and dharma. He is not just a historical figure or mythological hero but a living manifestation of truth itself. His life and actions offer timeless lessons on the values of integrity, duty, and virtue. Rama's commitment to truth is unwavering, even when faced with immense trials and personal sacrifices. In his journey, he shows that following the path of truth is not always the easiest, but it is always the noblest. Rama's choices were guided by dharma—righteous action—and he demonstrated through his actions that truth is not a mere concept but a force that shapes reality.

Rama's devotion to dharma is seen in his ability to make decisions based on the highest ethical standards, regardless of personal pain or hardship. His exile to the forest, the sacrifice of his kingdom, and his unwavering adherence to his principles even in the face of betrayal all speak to the profound depth of his commitment to truth. For Rama, truth was not a relative notion—it was the foundation of his existence, something to be upheld at any cost. Through his character, he reveals that living in alignment with the truth of one's purpose leads to true peace and fulfilment.

In spiritual terms, Rama is often referred to as "Maryada Purushottama," the supreme being who sets the boundaries of righteousness and moral conduct. His life exemplifies the essence of dharma—maintaining balance and harmony in the world while remaining true to one's higher calling. By embodying truth in every aspect of his life, Rama teaches us that we too can overcome adversity and live a life of virtue.

Just as the sun's light illuminates the world, the truth embodied by Rama lights the way for all those who seek guidance. His legacy continues to inspire millions, reminding us that living by the truth—no matter the circumstance—brings us closer to the divine and reveals the eternal wisdom of the universe.

**** ** ****

Swamy, you once said,

"Truth is Rama, Truth is God."

Why do you mention only Rama in this context, and not Krishna, Jesus, or Bala Tripura? Is there a specific intention or context behind choosing Rama to represent Truth? Please explain so that we may understand the deeper meaning behind these words.

Swamy's Spirit Speaks:

Child, when I declare **"Truth is Rama, Truth is God,"** I am using the name "Rama" as a symbol—a luminous emblem of righteousness, integrity, and the unwavering commitment to truth. In our spiritual heritage, Rama is revered not merely as a historical figure, but as the embodiment of divine truth and dharma. His life, marked by virtue, honor, and compassion, serves as a timeless guide for living in accordance with the highest ideals.

Let me explain further:

- **Rama as the Embodiment of Truth:**

  - Rama exemplifies an ideal of truth that is clear, steadfast, and free from ego.

  - He stands as a model for all who seek to live righteously—his name conveys not only personal virtue but the universal quality of truth itself.

  - By saying **"Truth is Rama,"** I encourage you to see that the truth you seek is not abstract or distant; it is embodied in the virtues that Rama represents.

- **Why Not Other Names?**

  - You may wonder why I do not invoke Krishna, Jesus, or Bala Tripura. Each of these revered names indeed represents aspects of the Divine:

    - **Krishna** shines with playful wisdom and divine love.

    - **Jesus** embodies sacrificial love and redemption.

    - **Bala Tripura** reveals the creative and nurturing facets of the Divine.

  - However, in this context, I choose **Rama** because his example focuses on the resolute adherence to truth and the unwavering pursuit of dharma.

  - Rama's life teaches us that truth is not a matter of opinion or interpretation—it is an unchangeable, guiding light. When you align with truth, you are aligning with the Divine, irrespective of the form in which it appears.

- **The Universal Essence:**

  - Understand that whether you call upon Rama, Krishna, Jesus, or any other name, the essence remains the same: **Truth is God.**

  - Each name points to the same ultimate reality, expressed through different qualities and teachings.

  - My mention of Rama is intended to highlight a particular aspect of that truth—namely, its clarity, its commitment to righteousness, and its role as a beacon for ethical living.

Child, let these words inspire you to seek the truth within yourself, to see that truth as a divine light that guides every action, every thought, and every moment of your life. In doing so, you will realize that all paths, though varied in form, lead to the same eternal reality.

May you always remain steadfast in the pursuit of truth, and may the divine light of righteousness shine upon your path.

Chapter-16
The Outer Shell, Inner Core

The concept of "Inner vs. Outer" speaks to the dichotomy between our inner world—our thoughts, emotions, and spirit—and the outer world—our external circumstances, relationships, and material possessions. In today's fast-paced society, much of our focus tends to be on the outer world. We become preoccupied with our achievements, appearances, and material success, often overlooking the deeper, more meaningful aspects of our existence. The outer world is often in flux, influenced by external forces beyond our control. It can be tempting to base our sense of happiness and fulfilment on outer achievements and validations, but this approach is often fleeting and unstable.

The inner world, on the other hand, is where true peace, wisdom, and strength reside. Our thoughts, beliefs, and emotional state shape how we experience the world around us. When we look inward, we connect with our higher self, our purpose, and our deeper understanding of life. The inner world is constant and unchanging, providing a solid foundation for navigating the ever-changing outer world. True contentment does not come from external possessions or recognition, but from cultivating peace, balance, and clarity within ourselves.

Spiritual teachings often emphasize the importance of nurturing the inner world, as it is through self-awareness, self-reflection, and inner growth that we are able to transcend the superficial aspects of life. When we align our inner world with our outer actions, we create harmony between the two. The true path to happiness lies not in the accumulation of external wealth or status, but in the cultivation of inner peace, wisdom, and compassion. By turning inward, we find that the external world loses its power to control us. We begin to see beyond the distractions, focusing instead on living in alignment with our authentic self and with the greater truth that binds us all. In this way, the inner and outer worlds are not separate, but interconnected—and by mastering the inner, we shape a more fulfilling outer life.

**** ** ****

Swamy, you once stated,

"Compare inside and outside power and status, don't compare. Don't copy. Compose yourself."

These words are both instructive and thought-provoking. While they sound educative, I feel there is a deeper, unique message behind them. Could you please explain what you mean by this, so that we may understand the inner essence and apply it in our lives?

Swamy's Spirit Speaks:

Child, these words are meant to guide you away from the pitfalls of external validation and toward the nurturing of your inner self. Let me break down the message for you:

- **"Compare inside and outside power and status"**

  - **Outside Power and Status:**

    In the world, society often measures worth by external factors—wealth, influence, titles, and appearances. These are fleeting and can create feelings of inadequacy or superiority when you compare yourself with others.

  - **Inside Power and Status:**

    Your true strength and worth come from within. This inner power is built on virtues such as wisdom, compassion, integrity, and self-awareness. It is the enduring, unchanging essence of who you are.

- **"Don't compare. Don't copy."**

  - **Avoid Comparison:**

    When you compare yourself with others, you invite dissatisfaction and envy. Each person's journey is unique, and no external measure can capture the richness of your inner experience.

  - **Avoid Imitation:**

    To copy another's way of life is to deny your own individuality. Authentic growth comes from embracing your unique qualities rather than mimicking someone else's path.

- **"Compose Yourself."**

  - This is an invitation to create and nurture your own inner harmony.

  - **Compose Yourself** means to gather your thoughts, align your actions with your inner truth, and build a life that reflects your unique potential.

  - It is about finding balance and integrity within, so that your external actions naturally flow from a well-cultivated inner world.

The Inner Essence:

Child, the essence of my words is a call to prioritize your inner development over superficial measures of success.

- Recognize that true power lies in the inner self—the qualities that remain constant despite the ever-changing external world.

- Do not allow the world's transient standards to dictate your worth. Instead, nurture and develop your unique strengths and virtues.

- When you compose yourself, you become the author of your own life, guided by inner truth rather than by the shifting opinions of others.

May you always strive to build your inner world with care and let your authentic self shine, unburdened by comparison or imitation.

Chapter-17

The Sacred Path of Directions

In spiritual teachings, directions often symbolize more than just physical pathways or geographical bearings; they represent the flow of energy, wisdom, and divine guidance in our lives. The sacred path of directions is a metaphor for the spiritual journey that we all embark upon. Each direction— North, South, East, and West—holds its own significance and invites us to explore different aspects of our existence and consciousness. These directions are not just physical orientations but are symbolic of the spiritual and internal realms we navigate in our pursuit of truth.

The East, often associated with the rising sun, symbolizes the dawn of enlightenment and new beginnings. It is the direction of birth and renewal, the place where divine wisdom enters our lives. In this space, we are invited to cultivate spiritual awareness, seeking the truth that illuminates our path. The South, associated with warmth and nurturing, teaches us the importance of growth, compassion, and love. This direction encourages us to connect with our hearts, nurturing relationships and fostering empathy and kindness in our actions. The West, where the sun sets, reminds us of the cycles of life and death, and the importance of transformation and release. It calls us to embrace impermanence and to let go of attachments that hinder our growth, preparing us for the spiritual rebirth that awaits. Finally, the North is often seen as the direction of wisdom, strength, and stability. It represents the inner strength we cultivate through discipline and dedication, providing us with the foundation to continue our journey with resilience and grace.

In a spiritual sense, the sacred path of directions teaches us how to balance the various aspects of life—our mind, heart, body, and soul. It calls us to align our actions with the principles of dharma, to move forward with integrity, and to honor the sacredness in all things. The journey is not a linear one; rather, it is cyclical, where each direction offers its lessons, guiding us toward wholeness. By understanding and embracing these directions, we are reminded that life is a sacred path—one that requires our attention, our mindfulness, and our connection to the divine presence that resides within us and around us. Ultimately, the sacred path of directions leads us to discover our true purpose and divine essence, helping us find peace and fulfilment in every step we take.

** ** **

Swamy, you often speak of directions by saying,

"North and East are Positive Directions, South is Negative, and West is Neutral."

My question is: if God resides in all directions, why should there be such deviations or distractions? Please explain.

Swamy's Spirit Speaks:

Child, the statement about directions is not a literal division of the Divine but a symbolic guide to the different energetic qualities that influence our lives. Let me explain:

- **Symbolic Significance of the Directions:**
  - **North and East as Positive:**
    - The East, where the sun rises, symbolizes new beginnings, illumination, and inspiration.
    - The North represents stability, wisdom, and a steady progression toward higher truth.
    - Together, these directions remind you to seek and align with energies that uplift and inspire you.

- **South as Negative:**
  - The South, symbolically, points to challenges and obstacles.
  - It represents the forces that pull you downward, the trials that test your strength and resolve.
  - However, these challenges are opportunities for growth—they are the pressures that refine your inner self, much like fire purifies gold.

- **West as Neutral:**
  - The West signifies balance—a space where both light and shadow coexist.
  - It encourages you to reflect on your experiences without bias, helping you to integrate the lessons of both success and struggle.

- **The Universal Presence of God:**
  - Although these directions symbolize different energies, remember that **God is omnipresent and transcends all these boundaries.**
  - The Divine resides in every direction and every aspect of creation; these symbols are simply tools to help you understand and balance the various influences in your life.

- **Navigating Life's Energies:**
  - Use the positive energies of the North and East as your guiding lights to inspire and motivate you.
  - Recognize the lessons in the challenges of the South as opportunities to grow stronger and wiser.
  - Embrace the neutrality of the West to cultivate balance and clarity in your perceptions.
  - These distinctions are not meant to limit your understanding of the Divine but to offer you a framework for living in harmony with the dynamic flow of life.

Child, while it may seem that these directional qualities impose limitations, they are only symbolic markers that help you discern the energies around you. In truth, **the Divine is one, unbounded by any direction, yet it expresses itself in myriad ways through these natural symbols.**

May you always see beyond the symbols to the infinite light that pervades all, and may you find balance and wisdom in every direction of your journey.

BREAKING CONDITIONED PATTERNS

(Shedding Past Conditioning and Social Norms to
discover authentic nature)

Chapter-18

Balance for Bliss

Spiritual balance is the harmony between our inner and outer worlds. It is about finding peace in our heart and mind, despite the chaos that may surround us. Just as a tree stands tall and firm, rooted in the earth, yet reaches out freely to the sky, spiritual balance is about being grounded in your values and faith, while also being open to growth and change. It's not about escaping the challenges of life but learning to navigate them with grace, using them as stepping stones to deeper wisdom and understanding.

When we achieve spiritual balance, we experience a sense of inner bliss, not because everything around us is perfect, but because we have learned to embrace life's ebb and flow. This balance comes from recognizing that every experience—both joyful and challenging—serves a purpose in our spiritual journey. By practicing mindfulness, devotion, and self-awareness, we create a space where peace, clarity, and bliss can flow freely, regardless of external circumstances. True bliss comes not from seeking happiness outside of ourselves but from realizing that it already resides within, waiting for us to find balance and connect with it.

** ** **

Swamy, you once said while addressing a group of visitors,

"Over talk and over thought will override your life, balance talk and balanced thought will bring bounty of bliss."

I understand that excessive talking and thinking can be harmful, but please explain the deeper, inner essence of these words in your unique way so that I may truly grasp their significance.

Swamy's Spirit Speaks:

Child, these words are a gentle yet profound reminder that the quality of your inner life directly influences the quality of your outer existence. Let me break down the essence for you:

- **Over Talk and Over Thought:**

    - When you engage in excessive talking, you scatter your energy in endless chatter, often drowning out the silence needed for inner reflection.

    - Overthinking, likewise, creates a storm of restless mental activity that can overwhelm and confuse the heart.

    - Both these extremes, when left unchecked, override the natural balance of your life, leaving you disconnected from your inner truth.

- **Balanced Talk and Balanced Thought:**

    - **Balanced talk** means speaking with purpose, clarity, and mindful restraint. It is about expressing yourself in a way that is both honest and measured, allowing your words to uplift rather than create noise.

    - **Balanced thought** is the art of reflective meditation—where you allow ideas to surface gently, examine them with clarity, and then let them pass, maintaining a serene mind.

    - In balance, your communication and thought become aligned with your inner wisdom, creating space for genuine insight and peace.

- **Bounty of Bliss:**

    - When you achieve this equilibrium, you tap into a deeper reservoir of joy and inner fulfilment.

    - Your mind becomes a wellspring of clarity, and your words carry the light of truth. This, in turn, attracts harmonious relationships, opportunities for growth, and a sense of overall well-being.

- The "bounty of bliss" is not a fleeting pleasure; it is the sustained, rich fulfilment that arises when your inner and outer worlds are in harmonious alignment.

Child, the true essence of my words is to encourage you to cultivate mindfulness in both speech and thought. By doing so, you not only avoid the pitfalls of excessive mental chatter and idle talk but also create a fertile ground for inner peace and spiritual growth.

May you always strive to find the perfect balance so that your life is filled with the abundant, lasting joy that comes from living in harmony with your inner truth.

Chapter-19
Balanced Approach

In the rush of modern life, it's easy to get caught up in extremes—whether it's striving too hard for success, overindulging in pleasures, or becoming overwhelmed by stress. Yet, true peace and fulfilment lie in balance. A balanced approach is about aligning the mind, body, and spirit in harmony, ensuring that none of these elements dominates the others. It is the understanding that every aspect of life requires attention and care, but none should be neglected or overemphasized. Just as a well-tuned instrument produces beautiful music, a balanced life creates a symphony of peace, health, and joy.

Living with balance doesn't mean avoiding challenges or emotions; rather, it means responding to them with wisdom and grace. It's about making choices that nurture all areas of your life—work, relationships, health, and spirituality—without tipping the scale too far in one direction. A balanced approach teaches us to embrace both the light and dark, the joys and struggles, recognizing that both are integral to our growth. In this way, we become more resilient, grounded, and aware of the present moment. Ultimately, a balanced approach is about living authentically, accepting life's impermanence, and finding contentment in the flow of it all.

** ** **

Swamy, your way of expression, though jovial, carries a heavy weight of wisdom that urges reflection and action. On one occasion, you said,

"Be like a dog. Don't become a monkey, carry like a donkey, don't run like a horse, don't expand but extend."

This statement means a great deal, yet I find it difficult to fully comprehend its depth. Could you please explain its inner essence so that I may explore and apply its message in my life?

Swamy's Spirit Speaks:

Child, this metaphorical guidance is designed to help you navigate life's complexities by cultivating humility, persistence, and purposeful growth. Let me break it down for you:

- **"Be like a dog":**
  - A dog embodies loyalty, humility, and devoted service without expectation of praise.
  - This is an invitation to develop unwavering commitment and sincere love in your actions.
  - Emulate the dog's readiness to serve and its steadfastness in building deep, genuine relationships.

- **"Don't become a monkey":**
  - A monkey, though playful, represents restlessness, superficiality, and a tendency to be distracted by trivial pursuits.
  - I caution you against indulging in vanity, mischief, or the endless chase of fleeting pleasures.
  - Instead, focus on cultivating a calm and focused mind that does not get easily diverted by the noise of the world.

- **"Carry like a donkey":**
  - A donkey is known for its perseverance, reliability, and its ability to bear burdens steadily over time.
  - This metaphor encourages you to shoulder your responsibilities with endurance and a humble spirit.
  - It is about accepting life's challenges with quiet strength, without complaint, and with a willingness to persist no matter how heavy the load may be.

- **"Don't run like a horse":**

  - A horse is swift and energetic, but its speed can lead to impulsive and unthinking actions.

  - I advise you not to let your enthusiasm turn into reckless haste.

  - Instead, move forward with deliberate care, ensuring that every step is thoughtful and balanced.

- **"Don't expand but extend":**

  - To "expand" often means to grow without direction or control—an uncontrolled burst that may lose focus.

  - In contrast, "extend" suggests a purposeful reach, a gentle yet steady expansion of your capabilities, service, and love.

  - This means sharing your true self with others, reaching out in a way that is meaningful and considerate, rather than simply accumulating more without purpose.

The Inner Essence:

Child, the overall teaching is to adopt a balanced approach in life:

- **Embrace the loyalty and selfless service of a dog.**

- **Avoid the distractions and superficiality symbolized by the monkey.**

- **Take on life's burdens with the steady endurance of a donkey.**

- **Resist the urge for impulsive action like that of a horse.**

- **And instead of uncontrolled growth, aim to extend your true potential and compassion purposefully.**

By integrating these qualities, you will navigate your life with humility, resilience, and clarity. Your inner strength and character will shine through, guiding you to make choices that lead to a life of profound fulfilment and service.

May you always walk the path with balanced courage and gentle determination, and may your actions reflect the deep wisdom that lies within you.

Chapter-20

Balance of Wealth and Wisdom

Wealth and wisdom are often seen as separate pursuits—one focused on material gain and the other on intellectual or spiritual growth. However, when balanced, they complement each other, creating a harmonious life that nurtures both the mind and the soul. Wealth, in its truest sense, is not just about accumulation; it is about using resources to enrich not only our own lives but the lives of others. Wisdom, on the other hand, teaches us to recognize the fleeting nature of material things and encourages us to use our wealth thoughtfully and compassionately. When wealth is guided by wisdom, it becomes a tool for greater good, leading to prosperity not just in financial terms but in relationships, experiences, and personal growth.

Achieving balance between wealth and wisdom is an act of conscious living. It requires understanding that material success, while important, is not the ultimate goal of life. True wealth lies in the ability to live with purpose, integrity, and generosity. Wisdom helps us see beyond the temporary, to understand what is truly valuable and sustainable in life. It shows us that wealth is a means, not an end, and that its greatest power is in how it is used. By aligning wealth with wisdom, we avoid the pitfalls of greed and excess, instead fostering a life that is rich in meaning, connection, and fulfilment.

In the spiritual realm, wealth is not defined by possessions, but by the abundance of knowledge, love, and service we share. Wisdom guides us to recognize that every material possession is temporary, and true wealth is found in cultivating inner peace, compassion, and a sense of purpose. The balance of wealth and wisdom is about living in harmony with the world around us—using what we have to create a better world, while remaining grounded in the understanding that our true worth lies in who we are, not what we own.

**** ** ****

Swamy, you once shared the story of the Cat and the Rat, and during our interaction, you suddenly said,

"Become cat before Rat, become rat before cat, cat means wealth, rat means wisdom."

I wish to understand the deeper meaning behind these words. Could you please explain their inner essence in your unique way so that my perceptions may broaden?

Swamy's Spirit Speaks:

Child, the story of the Cat and the Rat is a metaphor for the interplay between two essential qualities: the dynamic drive to create abundance and the subtle wisdom required to navigate life.

- **"Become cat before Rat":**
  - The **cat** symbolizes qualities of assertiveness, resourcefulness, and the ability to attract wealth—not only material but also the wealth of opportunities and experiences.
  - To **become cat** is to cultivate ambition, confidence, and the drive to pursue your goals energetically.
  - It teaches you to take bold action, to seize the moment, and to harness the power of creation with clarity and purpose.
- **"Become rat before cat":**
  - The **rat** represents wisdom, adaptability, and keen observation.

- To **become rat** means to develop a sharp, discerning mind that notices the smallest details and learns from every situation.

- The rat's energy is about humility, curiosity, and the quiet accumulation of knowledge that guides you in making wise decisions.

- **Interplay and Balance:**

  - These instructions are not contradictory; rather, they urge you to balance two complementary forces in your life.

  - At times, you must harness the assertiveness and dynamic energy of the cat to attract abundance. In other moments, you need the subtle, reflective qualities of the rat to gain wisdom and insight.

  - The true mastery of life lies in knowing when to embody each quality and, ultimately, in integrating them so that your actions are both effective and thoughtful.

- **The Broader Message:**

  - **Wealth and wisdom are not opposites but partners in the journey of life.**

  - True success comes when you can attract opportunities and resources like the cat while also discerning and adapting like the rat.

  - When these qualities coexist, you move through life with both strength and insight, achieving a harmonious balance that nourishes your body, mind, and soul.

Child, embrace the ambition of the cat and the insight of the rat. Learn to oscillate between creating and reflecting, acting boldly and observing keenly. In doing so, you will discover that the interplay of wealth and wisdom is the key to a truly balanced and enriched life.

May you always find the perfect harmony between these forces, and may your journey be one of continual growth, prosperity, and deep understanding.

Chapter-21

Recognition Through Reorganization

Recognition is often sought through achievement, titles, and accolades. However, true recognition often emerges when we choose to reorganize our priorities and perspectives. Reorganization is about realigning our thoughts, actions, and values with a higher purpose. It involves stepping back and reflecting on what truly matters—whether it's prioritizing our relationships, aligning with our inner truths, or dedicating ourselves to meaningful work. In this realignment, recognition is not dependent on external validation but is a natural outcome of living authentically and purposefully.

When we reorganize our lives around purpose, we begin to attract recognition in its purest form—the respect and admiration of others who see our commitment and integrity. This recognition is not about fame or status, but about the impact we have on those around us through our actions, our values, and our example. As we reorganize our priorities to reflect our true essence, we inspire others to do the same, creating a ripple effect of positive change.

Through reorganization, we move from seeking recognition to embodying it in our everyday lives, cultivating a deeper sense of fulfilment and harmony in the process.

** ** **

Swamy, you often mention,

"What is recognition? You re-organize your mind, recharge your mind, and automatically, you get recognition."

It sounds appealing, yet the process seems challenging. Could you please explain the deeper, inner message behind these words so that I may understand how re-organizing and recharging the mind naturally leads to genuine recognition?

Swamy's Spirit Speaks:

Child, this statement is a profound invitation to transform your inner world, so that true recognition—recognition that comes from within—flourishes effortlessly. Let me break down its essence for you:

- **Re-organize Your Mind:**

  This means to reset your mental framework.

  - Let go of disordered thoughts, limiting beliefs, and the clutter of negativity that obscures clarity.

  - By re-organizing, you create a clean slate where wisdom, purpose, and inner truth can shine forth.

  - When your mind is orderly, it becomes receptive to deeper insights and aligns with the natural flow of life.

- **Recharge Your Mind:**

  Like a battery that needs renewal, your mind requires fresh energy and inspiration.

  - Recharge it through practices such as meditation, self-reflection, and learning—activities that uplift and rejuvenate your inner spirit.

  - This recharging process infuses you with positive energy, making you resilient in the face of life's challenges.

- **Automatically You Get Recognition:**

  As your mind becomes both organized and recharged, you naturally radiate a unique inner brilliance.

  - This recognition is not something you force or seek externally; it arises as a natural consequence of your inner transformation.

- Others begin to notice the light within you—your clarity, compassion, and integrity—without you having to proclaim it.

- It is the genuine acknowledgment of your true self, emerging effortlessly from the harmony of your inner state.

The Inner Essence:

Child, the process is not about chasing after accolades or external approval. Rather, it is about cultivating a state of inner order and vitality that, in turn, reflects outwardly.

- **Re-organizing** clears away the confusion and establishes a foundation of clarity.

- **Recharging** replenishes your spirit with fresh, positive energy.

- Together, these actions transform your entire being, so that recognition—true, lasting, and divine—flows naturally, like light from a well-tended lamp.

Though the process may seem difficult, remember that every moment spent in nurturing your inner self is an investment in your spiritual evolution. As you refine your mind, you not only become a beacon of inspiration for yourself but also for all those around you.

May you find the strength and grace to continually re-organize and recharge your mind, and may the authentic recognition of your inner light guide you on your path to truth.

Chapter-22
Simplicity in Service

In a world that often values complexity, achievement, and grandeur, simplicity in service is a rare and profound expression of humility and grace. True service does not require grand gestures or complicated acts; rather, it thrives in the everyday moments when we choose to serve with an open heart and a selfless spirit. Simplicity in service is about offering our time, energy, and resources without expectation, and without the need for recognition or reward. It is the quiet act of helping others—whether through a kind word, a compassionate gesture, or a genuine listening ear—that has the power to create profound impact.

When we serve with simplicity, we connect with the essence of what it means to be human. We transcend the ego and remove the barriers that often separate us from others. In these humble acts, we experience the beauty of unconditional love and compassion. Simplicity in service is not about how much we give, but the intention behind our giving. It is about offering what we have—whether it's our skills, our resources, or simply our presence—in the spirit of generosity, kindness, and empathy. This kind of service is timeless and universal, touching the hearts of both the giver and the receiver.

In the spiritual realm, simplicity in service is often seen as the highest form of devotion. It is the recognition that true fulfilment does not come from accumulating wealth, titles, or accolades, but from being of service to others. By serving simply, we align ourselves with the divine, embodying the principle that all beings are interconnected and deserving of love and respect. The more we practice simplicity in service, the more we become vessels of peace and compassion in the world. This service does not seek to impress or to achieve anything, but to simply be present, offering ourselves freely and wholeheartedly to those in need.

In serving simply, we discover that true fulfilment comes not from the complexity of our actions, but from the purity of our intention. The simplicity of service allows us to experience the deepest joy and connection, reminding us that the greatest blessings in life often come from the most unassuming and humble acts.

** ** **

Swamy, I like very much what you said,

"Continue Simple Living, Continue Seva in a Simple Way."

Please explain the inner essence of these words and how they activate our spirit of living.

Swamy's Spirit Speaks:

Child, these words are a gentle invitation to embrace a life of clarity and compassion—a life where simplicity and selfless service become the very fabric of your being.

- **Simple Living:**
  - **Living Simply** means letting go of unnecessary complexities, material excess, and distractions that cloud your inner vision.
  - It is a call to focus on what truly matters: nurturing your inner self, building meaningful relationships, and aligning with the natural rhythms of life.
  - In simplicity, you create space for peace, clarity, and the divine spark that resides within you.

- **Seva (Selfless Service) in a Simple Way:**
  - **Seva** is the act of serving others without any expectation of reward or recognition.
  - To practice **seva simply** is to offer your help and compassion in the most natural, unpretentious manner.
  - It is a heartfelt expression of love, where the act of giving flows effortlessly from your inner abundance.
  - When you serve without pretense or ulterior motives, you mirror the selfless nature of the Divine.

- **Activating the Spirit of Living:**
  - When you embrace simple living, you unburden your mind and heart, allowing your true self to emerge.
  - In this clear state, your actions become more aligned with your inner truth, and you find that every moment carries the potential for growth and joy.
  - By engaging in simple seva, you transform your daily interactions into acts of grace. You contribute to the well-being of others, and in doing so, your spirit is uplifted and your life is enriched.
  - This harmonious blend of simplicity and service creates a cycle of inner fulfilment—each act of giving nurtures your soul, and each moment of clarity inspires more compassionate action.

Child, the essence of these words is not about renouncing the world but about engaging with it in a way that honors your true nature.

When you live simply, you make room for wisdom. When you serve simply, you allow love to shine through every action.

In this way, your life becomes a continuous celebration of the divine, and your spirit is activated to experience the profound beauty of existence.

May you always find the courage to live and the grace to serve selflessly so that your life becomes a beacon of light and love for all.

Chapter-23

The Dance of Energy

Attraction is a powerful force that governs much of our experience in the material and spiritual worlds. It draws us toward people, things, and experiences that resonate with us, whether consciously or unconsciously. This natural pull can be seen in the way we are attracted to relationships, passions, desires, and even ideas. Attraction often arises from our inner needs and desires, pulling us toward that which promises fulfilment or growth. However, while attraction is a force that enriches our lives, it can also lead us into imbalances if we become too fixated on the object of our desire. When we lack awareness, attraction can pull us off course, causing us to become attached to things that may not serve our highest good.

Balance, on the other hand, is the key to navigating the forces of attraction without losing ourselves. It is about maintaining equilibrium between our internal and external worlds, our desires and our responsibilities, our actions and our intentions. Balance allows us to engage with life's attractions while remaining grounded and centered. In spiritual practice, balance teaches us that we do not need to chase after every desire or succumb to every pull we feel. Instead, we can approach life with discernment, recognizing that not everything that attracts us is meant for us. Through balance, we learn to honor the things that nourish our soul and let go of the distractions that lead us astray.

Spiritual traditions often speak of the importance of balance in one's life—between the mind and heart, action and contemplation, worldly responsibilities and spiritual pursuits. It is through maintaining balance that we avoid being swept away by the currents of life, remaining anchored in our true nature. Just as a pendulum swings, attraction and balance are two complementary forces. The key to harmony lies not in avoiding attraction, but in knowing how to navigate it with awareness, self-control, and discernment. When we achieve this balance, we experience a deeper connection to ourselves and the universe, moving through life with purpose, clarity, and grace. In this way, attraction becomes not a source of distraction, but a tool for growth and evolution, helping us reach our fullest potential without losing sight of what truly matters.

**** ** ****

Swamy, you once stated,

"Don't attract to attack, attract to adjust, don't get attracted, attract to accuse."

I understand the meaning of each word on its own, but when they are combined, I find it confusing. What is the significance of this statement? Please explain its deeper essence so that even common spiritual aspirants can understand and apply it in their lives.

Swamy's Spirit Speaks:

Child, these words form a subtle guideline for channeling your inner energy and intentions when you encounter challenges. Let me unravel their meaning for you:

- **"Don't attract to attack":**

  - **Avoid provoking conflict:** Do not intentionally stir up anger or hostility.

  - **Focus on non-violence:** When you engage with the world, let your actions be gentle and non-combative.

- **Conserve your energy:** Rather than directing your strength toward harming or diminishing others, use it wisely.

- **"Attract to adjust":**

  - **Channel energy for positive change:** Direct your energy toward improving situations and adapting constructively.

  - **Self-correction:** Allow the challenges you face to guide you in making better choices and refining your character.

  - **Harmonize differences:** Use your influence to bring balance and resolution rather than deepening divisions.

- **"Don't get attracted":**

  - **Avoid being drawn into negativity:** Do not let external provocations or fleeting emotions pull you into a vortex of anger or resentment.

  - **Stay centered:** Keep your inner equilibrium intact by not reacting impulsively to every disturbance.

  - **Discernment is key:** Recognize that not every situation warrants your full emotional investment.

- **"Attract to accuse":**

  - **Hold accountable, but wisely:** If an injustice occurs, let your response be guided by fairness and clarity rather than blind blame.

  - **Constructive criticism:** Rather than indulging in endless accusations, focus on pointing out what needs correction with the aim of healing and improvement.

  - **Responsibility over retribution:** Ensure that any act of holding someone accountable comes from a place of integrity and the desire to restore balance—not from personal vendetta.

The Inner Essence:

Child, these words are a call to consciously manage your inner energies and reactions. They remind you to:

- **Act with Intention:**

  Be deliberate about where you direct your energy. Use it to adjust and improve, rather than to attack or to be swept away by negativity.

- **Maintain Inner Balance:**

  Cultivate a calm mind that is not easily disturbed by external conflicts. When you remain centred, you can respond rather than react impulsively.

- **Transform Challenges:**

  See every conflict as an opportunity to refine your character. Instead of succumbing to the urge to attack or accuse indiscriminately, use discernment to act in a way that promotes harmony and growth.

In short, **don't let the impulses of anger or blame dictate your actions; instead, choose to channel your energy towards constructive change and balanced accountability.** This is the path to a higher state of being—a state where your actions resonate with the deeper truth of non-violence, compassion, and inner harmony.

May you learn to direct your inner energy with wisdom and grace, transforming every challenge into an opportunity for growth and balance.

Chapter-24
The Pitfall of Attachment

Attachment is a fundamental part of the human experience, often rooted in our desire for security, love, and connection. At first glance, attachment may seem harmless, even necessary, as it shapes our relationships and emotional bonds. However, when taken too far, attachment can become a pitfall—an invisible trap that binds us to temporary things and fleeting experiences. We attach ourselves to people, objects, and outcomes, believing that our happiness and sense of worth are dependent on them. In doing so, we lose sight of the impermanence of life and the transient nature of the world around us.

The pitfall of attachment arises when we allow our identity and peace of mind to be defined by external factors. This dependence on external circumstances for happiness leads to suffering when those circumstances change, as they inevitably do. When the things we are attached to slip away or are no longer within our control, we experience loss, grief, and frustration. Instead of finding contentment in the present moment, we are constantly chasing after something, fearing its loss and clinging to it desperately when we find it. This cycle of attachment traps us in a state of craving and aversion, constantly seeking to hold on to what we desire while trying to push away what we fear.

Spiritual teachings often remind us that true peace and freedom lie in letting go of attachment. By releasing our grip on the things, people, and outcomes that we hold dear, we allow ourselves to experience the fullness of the

*present moment without the burden of expectation or fear.
Attachment, in this sense, prevents us from experiencing
life as it truly is—free, fluid, and ever-changing. It is through
detachment that we find true freedom. Detachment does not
mean withdrawing from life or abandoning our relationships;
rather, it is about cultivating an inner detachment from
the need to control or cling to anything.*

*When we embrace detachment, we are able to experience life
more fully, appreciating the beauty and joy in each moment
without the constant anxiety of attachment. We learn to flow
with the changes in life, trusting that all experiences—whether
pleasurable or painful—are part of the greater journey. True
freedom arises when we shift our focus from attachment to
inner contentment, realizing that the source of our peace and
happiness comes from within. Only then do we break free from
the pitfall of attachment and open ourselves to the boundless
joy and liberation that lie beyond.*

**** ** ****

Swamy, you once said,

"Don't establish, if you establish you will extract."

What is the meaning of this? What does it mean to establish, and why would establishing lead to extraction? Please explain the essence behind this statement so that I may understand its deeper significance.

Swamy's Spirit Speaks:

Child, this statement is a subtle reminder of the danger in trying to fix or rigidify what is naturally fluid and dynamic. Let me explain its inner essence:

- **To Establish:**
  - **Establishing** means setting something in a fixed form—creating boundaries, rigid structures, or inflexible systems.

- In the spiritual context, it can refer to the attempt to confine a dynamic truth or a natural process into a predetermined mould.

- When you try to **establish** the ever-changing flow of life or wisdom, you impose limitations on something that is meant to evolve freely.

- **To Extract:**

  - **Extraction** in this context means drawing out or stripping away the inherent, living essence of that which you try to fix.

  - When you establish something rigidly, you risk **extracting** its vitality, its spontaneous energy, and its true potential.

  - It is as if you force a vibrant, flowing river into a narrow canal—the water becomes constricted, losing its power and natural course.

- **The Deeper Message:**

  - The statement warns against the temptation to rigidly structure or confine the divine flow of life.

  - **Natural processes, like truth and energy, are dynamic; they flourish in openness and flexibility.**

  - When you attempt to set them into a fixed pattern, you inadvertently extract, or drain, their true power and beauty.

  - In practical terms, this means that if you cling too tightly to fixed ideas, dogmas, or rigid habits, you might miss the evolving wisdom that comes from embracing change and uncertainty.

Child, the wisdom here is to **allow the natural, living essence of truth and energy to flow freely.** Do not try to capture it in rigid forms, for in doing so, you diminish its potential. Instead, remain open and receptive, letting the dynamic process reveal its own beauty and strength.

May you learn to honour the fluid nature of life, embracing change and allowing your inner wisdom to unfold without the constraints of rigid establishment.

Chapter-25

Living with Purpose and Power

Living with purpose and power means aligning your actions with your values, and moving through life with intention. It is about waking up each day knowing why you are here and understanding the impact you can have. Purpose gives life direction, while power comes from within, fueled by the strength of your beliefs and the clarity of your goals. It's about owning your path, with a steady heart and mind, fully aware of your ability to shape your world.

When you live with purpose, you move with conviction, trusting in your ability to overcome challenges and stay true to your mission. This power isn't about force or control; it's the quiet confidence that arises when you are aligned with your true self. You radiate strength because you are driven by something greater than yourself, something that guides and supports you. Living with purpose and power means embracing your potential to inspire, create, and serve, and doing so with integrity and passion every day.

** ** **

Swamy, you once said,

"Lead a practical, perfect and powerful life."

I grasp the inner intention behind these words, yet I need more than a simple answer. What is the deeper, inner message behind this statement? How should we truly understand and embody a practical, perfect, and powerful life?

Swamy's Spirit Speaks:

Child, these words are a profound call to live in a way that integrates the everyday with the eternal. Let me reveal their inner essence:

- **Practical Life:**
  - To live practically is to remain grounded in reality—to understand and work with the world as it is, not as an illusion or mere abstraction.
  - It means engaging with your responsibilities, making wise decisions, and applying your knowledge with clarity and purpose.
  - This practicality is the soil in which your inner virtues can grow; it is the foundation upon which true transformation is built.

- **Perfect Life:**
  - Perfection here is not about flawlessness in the mundane sense but about aligning with your highest nature.
  - It is the realization that your true self is whole and complete, regardless of external imperfections.
  - When you live perfectly, you cultivate inner virtues—truth, compassion, and humility—that mirror the divine essence within you.
  - This inner perfection is a state of integrity, where your actions consistently reflect your inner wisdom.

- **Powerful Life:**
  - Power, in its truest sense, is not coercion or domination but the strength of inner resolve and clarity.
  - A powerful life is one where your energy is directed by conscious choice rather than by reactive impulses.
  - It is the ability to transform challenges into opportunities, to inspire others, and to radiate the light of your inner self.

- ○ This power emerges from disciplined practice, self-awareness, and an unwavering connection to the Divine.

The Integrated Message:

Child, when you lead a practical, perfect, and powerful life, you are not merely surviving—you are flourishing in alignment with your true purpose.

- **Practicality** grounds you in the reality of daily life, ensuring that your actions are wise and effective.

- **Perfection** reflects the cultivation of inner virtues, a constant reminder that your true essence is pure and whole.

- **Power** arises as you channel your inner strength to transform your life and the lives of those around you.

Together, these qualities enable you to navigate the world with clarity and confidence, while continually evolving toward the highest expression of your being. They remind you that every moment is an opportunity to realign with your inner truth, to act with purpose, and to radiate the divine light that resides within you.

May you strive always to embody these qualities, allowing your life to become a beacon of wisdom, compassion, and strength.

Chapter-26
Equilibrium

Equilibrium is the delicate dance between opposing forces—peace and chaos, joy and sorrow, action and rest. It is the ability to maintain balance amidst life's constant fluctuations. In a world full of distractions and demands, finding equilibrium is an act of mindfulness, a commitment to keeping ourselves centered despite external circumstances.

When we cultivate inner balance, we realize that true strength comes from harmony, not from extremes. Life is not about perfection, but about the grace to navigate through challenges with calm and clarity. Equilibrium allows us to be grounded in the present moment, balancing our desires and responsibilities, our emotions and thoughts. It is the ability to stay connected to our purpose while adapting to the changes that life brings.

Achieving equilibrium is not a one-time task, but a continuous process of self-awareness and adjustment. It is a reminder that when we align ourselves with the natural flow of life, we can experience true peace. In the midst of life's unpredictability, equilibrium offers us the power to stay balanced, focused, and at peace with ourselves.

** ** **

Swamy, you once said,

"Forget Home in Office and Office in Home."

This teaching is true in its essence, yet in today's society where work-from-home is common and boundaries often blur, people carry office work into their homes and vice versa, affecting their health and well-being. How can one create a clear separation between home and office life? Please explain the deeper meaning of this statement and how we can practically maintain this balance.

Swamy's Spirit Speaks:

Child, my words are a call to honour the natural boundaries that preserve your inner harmony. Let me explain:

- **The Essence of the Teaching:**

    - **"Forget Home in Office and Office in Home"** is a reminder that your sacred space of home and the demanding realm of work must remain distinct.

    - Home is your sanctuary—a place of rest, reflection, and nurturing relationships.

    - The office, or work, is the arena of duty and action where you perform your responsibilities.

    - When these two realms blend indiscriminately, your energy becomes scattered, and the balance of life is disturbed.

- **The Modern Challenge:**

    - In today's world, the boundaries between home and office often blur, especially with the rise of remote work.

    - This interchange can lead to constant stress, burnout, and even physical and mental health issues.

    - The challenge is to create a conscious separation that allows you to fully engage in work when needed, while also reclaiming personal time and space to rejuvenate.

- **Practical Ways to Maintain Separation:**

    - **Establish a Dedicated Workspace:**

        - Even if you work from home, designate a specific area solely for work.

- When you step into that space, it is time for professional activities; when you leave it, the workday ends.

- **Set Clear Boundaries and Routines:**

    - Define start and end times for your workday, and stick to them as much as possible.

    - This helps your mind understand when to switch modes—from the focused energy of work to the restful, nurturing energy of home.

- **Mindful Transitions:**

    - Create rituals to mark the transition between work and home.

    - For instance, a short meditation or a walk after work can signal your mind that it's time to shift from the active mode of the office to the calm space of home.

- **Digital Detox:**

    - Limit work-related communications after certain hours.

    - Allow yourself periods during the day when you disconnect from digital devices, so that the intrusion of work does not seep into your personal time.

- **Cultivate Inner Awareness:**

    - Practice mindfulness or meditation regularly to centre your thoughts.

    - This inner awareness helps you recognize when work stress is encroaching upon your home life and enables you to gently redirect your focus.

- **The Deeper Message:**

    - By maintaining distinct realms for work and personal life, you preserve the sanctity of your home as a space for regeneration and joy.

- This separation is not about rejecting duty or ambition, but about protecting your inner peace, which is essential for long-term productivity and happiness.

- In honoring these boundaries, you also acknowledge that every part of your life has its own energy and purpose.

- Ultimately, when you preserve this balance, your work becomes more focused and efficient, and your personal life more fulfilling and nurturing.

Child, I urge you to cultivate these boundaries with care. In doing so, you not only protect your health and spirit, but also enhance your capacity to perform your duties with greater clarity and enthusiasm.

May you always find the wisdom to create a harmonious balance between your professional and personal realms, and may your life be a testament to the beauty of living with purpose and peace.

Chapter-27

Align with Energy

Aligning with energy means connecting with the natural flow of life. It's about tuning into the positive energy around us and allowing it to guide us. When we align ourselves with good energy—whether it's through our thoughts, actions, or the people we interact with—we feel more focused, at ease, and in tune with our purpose. Just like a river moves smoothly when there are no obstacles, our lives move forward with ease when we embrace the right energy. By choosing what nourishes and uplifts us, we invite growth, peace, and new opportunities into our lives. Aligning with energy helps us create a life full of purpose and positivity.

** ** **

Swamy, you once said,

"Be aware that some enormous energy is working you; accept that energy, analyze that energy, act according to that energy, adjust with that energy, don't accuse that energy."

I understand that a mystic force is at work within and through me, for without that force, I am nothing. Yet, I still face inner dilemmas about how to relate to this powerful energy. Could you please explain the deeper meaning of these words to help clarify my inner doubts?

Swamy's Spirit Speaks:

Child, these words point to the cosmic force that animates all life—a force so vast and dynamic that it shapes your every thought, action, and experience. Let me share the essence of this teaching:

- **"Be aware that some enormous energy is working you":**
  - This is an invitation to recognize that beyond your individual identity, there is a universal, powerful energy at work in you and through you.
  - It is the force that infuses life into every cell, the subtle current that drives the evolution of your spirit.
  - Awareness of this energy is the first step to understanding that you are not an isolated self, but a part of a grand, interconnected cosmos.

- **"Accept that energy":**
  - Acceptance means acknowledging that this mystic force is an integral part of your existence.
  - Instead of resisting or denying its presence—perhaps out of fear or uncertainty—embrace it fully.
  - By accepting this energy, you open yourself to the flow of divine grace and allow transformation to begin.

- **"Analyze that energy":**
  - Analyze not in a cold, detached manner, but with a curious and discerning heart.
  - Observe how this energy influences your thoughts, your emotions, and your actions.
  - Reflect on its patterns and understand that it can be both creative and challenging—an ever-present guide on your spiritual journey.

- **"Act according to that energy":**
  - Once you have recognized and understood this force, align your actions with its natural flow.
  - Let it inform your choices and guide your responses to life's challenges, so that you move in harmony with the greater cosmic rhythm.

- ○ Acting in sync with this energy transforms your efforts into meaningful contributions to your growth and the well-being of others.

- **"Adjust with that energy":**

  - ○ Adjustment is the art of flexibility. As the energy in your life ebbs and flows, learn to adapt without losing your inner balance.

  - ○ When you adjust, you let go of rigid expectations and allow the dynamic force of life to mold you, bringing out the best in you.

- **"Don't accuse that energy":**

  - ○ Finally, do not blame this force for the challenges you face.

  - ○ Instead of accusing it for hardships or obstacles, understand that every manifestation—pleasant or painful—carries a lesson meant to refine you.

  - ○ Accusation only creates resistance and blocks the path of transformation.

  - ○ Embrace every experience as a vital part of your evolution.

Child, the mystic force that works through you is the very essence of life and creation. Remember, **you are not separate from this energy; you are its expression.** Without it, you are nothing, but with it, you become an ever-evolving miracle of divine potential.

May you always be open to the flow of this great energy, accept it with humility, and let it guide your actions and adjustments. In doing so, you will find that your inner dilemmas transform into stepping stones toward deeper wisdom and spiritual liberation.

Chapter-28

Remember and Pray

In the hustle and bustle of daily life, it's easy to lose sight of what truly matters. Remembering and praying offer us a chance to reconnect with our higher selves and the divine. To remember is to reflect on the moments that have shaped us—our blessings, our lessons, and our purpose. Prayer becomes a bridge to something greater, a sacred space where we can express gratitude, surrender our worries, and seek guidance.

Through prayer, we not only ask but also listen, aligning ourselves with a deeper wisdom that leads us toward clarity and peace. It's in these quiet moments of remembrance and prayer that we find strength beyond our own, grounding ourselves in love, faith, and hope. By embracing this simple yet profound practice, we invite transformation into our lives and open the door to healing, balance, and inner peace.

** ** **

Swamy, you once asked someone to bless themselves on the eve of their birthday by saying,

"What is Birthday? Birth day means—Remember the past, work for the present, pray for the future."

These words carry a profound, deeper meaning. Could you please explain what you mean by this and how one can understand and apply it in their life?

Swamy's Spirit Speaks:

Child, a birthday is not merely the celebration of the day you were born; it is a symbolic marker of your journey through life. The phrase "Remember the past, work for the present, pray for the future" encapsulates a holistic approach to living—a way to align your inner self with the flow of time. Let me break it down for you:

- **Remember the Past:**
  - **Reflection and Gratitude:**

    The past is a repository of your experiences—both the joys and the lessons from your challenges.

    - Reflect on what has been learned, appreciate the blessings that have shaped you, and recognize how your journey has contributed to your growth.

    - This remembrance is not about dwelling in regret, but about extracting wisdom from your experiences to guide you onward.

- **Work for the Present:**
  - **Active Engagement:**

    The present moment is the only time you truly have.

    - Working for the present means living fully in the "now"—engaging in your duties, nurturing relationships, and contributing positively to your surroundings.

    - It is about taking action with mindful intent and dedication, ensuring that your efforts in the moment build a foundation for a better future.

  - **Mindfulness and Productivity:**

    When you focus on the present, you harmonize your actions with your inner purpose, transforming each moment into an opportunity for growth and fulfilment.

- **Pray for the Future:**
  - **Faith and Aspiration:**

    Praying for the future is an act of surrender and hope.

    - It is about seeking divine guidance, trusting that higher wisdom will illuminate your path, and opening your heart to possibilities beyond your control.

    - This prayer is not a passive wish but a dynamic commitment to nurturing a future filled with peace, prosperity, and spiritual evolution.

  - **Setting Intentions:**

    When you pray, you set positive intentions that help steer your life toward the future you envision, aligning your inner will with the divine plan.

The Deeper Essence:

Child, a birthday reminds you that life is an ongoing cycle of growth, reflection, and aspiration.

- **By remembering the past,** you honor your journey and learn valuable lessons that prepare you for what lies ahead.

- **By working for the present,** you invest your energy in the here and now, creating the conditions for success and joy.

- **By praying for the future,** you maintain faith in the unseen forces that guide your destiny, opening yourself to grace and transformation.

This integrated approach to life is a gentle call to live consciously and fully. It encourages you to draw strength from your experiences, act with purposeful presence, and nurture hope for what is yet to come.

May you always find the wisdom to reflect, the courage to act, and the grace to trust in the unfolding of your life, so that each birthday becomes a celebration of your ever-deepening connection with the Divine.

Chapter-29

Renew and Realize

Life's beauty lies in its ever-changing nature, and with every cycle of change, there is an opportunity to renew and realize our deeper potential. To renew is not just about starting over, but about shedding the old layers that no longer serve us. It's a conscious decision to embrace growth, to clear the clutter in our minds and hearts, and make room for something more aligned with our true selves.

Renewal comes from within, allowing us to reawaken to the present moment and rediscover the power of fresh beginnings. It's through this inner renewal that we realize the vast potential lying dormant in us, waiting to be unleashed. Every setback, every challenge is an opportunity to transform, to learn, and to evolve. The process of realizing our true power is not about perfection, but about recognizing the wisdom we gain from each experience and using it to move forward with clarity and purpose.

As we renew, we step into a flow that connects us with the universe's endless possibilities. Through renewal, we come to understand that life is not something to control but something to embrace. By realizing the divine rhythm of this cycle, we unlock the freedom to evolve, transforming ourselves in ways we never imagined.

** ** **

Swamy, in another context you said,

"Birthday means, Recharge, Rechange, Reequip, Retain, Realize and Reach to Relax."

These words are wonderfully inspiring, but I would like to know what you actually mean by them. Do they encourage us to live with purpose, clarity, and resourcefulness? Please explain the deeper essence of this message.

Swamy's Spirit Speaks:

Child, these words are a roadmap for renewing and transforming your inner life, much like the celebration of a birthday marks a new beginning. Each term is a step in the process of aligning with your true self and the Divine. Allow me to explain:

- **Recharge:**
  - This means to restore your energy and vitality.
  - Just as a battery is recharged, you must regularly replenish your spirit through prayer, meditation, and moments of quiet reflection.
  - When you recharge, you prepare yourself to face life's challenges with a renewed inner strength.

- **Rechange:**
  - To rechange is to transform or convert.
  - It is about embracing change in your life and allowing old patterns to give way to new, higher possibilities.
  - This transformation is a sign of growth—each new cycle brings fresh opportunities to evolve.

- **Reequip:**
  - This step calls for gathering the tools, knowledge, and skills necessary for your journey.
  - Just as a warrior reequips before battle, you must continuously update your inner resources—your wisdom, compassion, and resilience—to navigate life's complexities.

- **Retain:**
  - To retain means to preserve and hold onto what is essential.
  - It involves safeguarding the virtues, lessons, and insights you acquire along the way.
  - By retaining these inner treasures, you build a stable foundation for continued growth.

- **Realize:**
  - Realizing is the awakening to your true nature.
  - It is the moment when you discern the deeper truth of your being and understand your place in the cosmic order.
  - This realization is the spark that ignites your inner clarity and transforms your perception of life.

- **Reach to Relax:**
  - Finally, "reach to relax" is the culmination of this inner work—attaining a state of deep peace and contentment.
  - It means that by following these steps, you gradually dissolve inner tension and allow your mind and heart to settle into a state of serene balance.
  - In that relaxed state, you are fully aligned with your purpose, and life flows with effortless grace.

The Deeper Essence:

Child, this message is an invitation to renew yourself continually. A birthday is not just a celebration of the past but a fresh start—a time to:

- **Recharge** your inner energy so that you can face each day with renewed vigor.

- **Rechange** your habits and patterns, letting go of what no longer serves you.

- **Reequip** yourself with the wisdom and tools necessary for your journey.

- **Retain** the valuable lessons and virtues that define your true self.

- **Realize** the deeper truth of who you are and your connection with the Divine.

- **Reach to relax,** achieving a state of inner calm and balance that allows you to live with purpose, clarity, and resourcefulness.

When you embody this process, you transform each moment into an opportunity for spiritual renewal, allowing your life to flourish with the brightness of new beginnings.

May you always find the strength to renew yourself and the grace to live in harmony with your true purpose.

Chapter-30

The Phoenix Within (Reflect and Rise)

In the hustle of daily life, it's easy to get caught up in the rush, forgetting to pause and reflect. Yet, the power of reflection lies in its ability to offer clarity and insight into our actions, thoughts, and emotions. When we take a moment to reflect, we gain perspective on where we are and where we want to go, helping us to make better choices and align with our true purpose.

Reflecting is not about dwelling on past mistakes or regrets, but about learning from them and using those lessons to rise higher. It's in these moments of quiet introspection that we uncover our strengths, acknowledge our growth, and identify areas for improvement. Through self-reflection, we unlock the potential to evolve, becoming more aware, more compassionate, and more resilient.

To rise is to take the wisdom gained from reflection and use it as a springboard for transformation. It's the willingness to embrace change and rise above challenges, knowing that each experience is an opportunity to grow. By reflecting and rising, we allow ourselves to break free from limitations and step into a brighter, more empowered version of who we are meant to be.

** ** **

Swamy, you often say,

"Look down, go up, look back, gain forward."

This phrase is truly wonderful, yet I find it challenging to understand how to put it into practice. Is there a way to do it, and what are the implications if we do not follow this guidance? Although I grasp a glimpse of its meaning, please share your wisdom so that I may fully comprehend and apply it.

Swamy's Spirit Speaks:

Child, this saying is a roadmap for continuous self-improvement and spiritual evolution. It encourages you to navigate life with humility, reflection, and purposeful action. Let me explain each part in detail:

- **"Look down":**

  - This invites you to humble yourself and observe your inner self.

  - To "look down" is to acknowledge your limitations, the impurities of the ego, and the areas in your life that require cleansing.

  - It is a call for introspection—recognize your shortcomings without harsh judgment, so you may learn from them.

- **"Go up":**

  - Once you have recognized your inner state by looking down, you are encouraged to rise from that introspection with renewed strength.

  - "Go up" means to elevate your consciousness by cultivating virtues such as compassion, wisdom, and courage.

  - This upward movement is the active process of transforming the insights you gain into higher, more refined actions.

- **"Look back":**

  - To "look back" is to reflect on your past experiences, the lessons you have learned, and even the mistakes you have made.

- It is an opportunity to assess your journey—understanding what worked, what didn't, and how you have grown over time.

- Through reflection, you gather wisdom that prepares you for the next step of your evolution.

- **"Gain forward":**

  - Finally, "gain forward" urges you to take the lessons from your introspection and reflection and use them as stepping stones toward your future.

  - It is about moving ahead with the newfound wisdom and strength, continuously improving and expanding your life's purpose.

  - This forward motion is not just physical progress but an inner evolution that enriches your entire being.

The Deeper Essence and Implications:

- **A Continuous Cycle:**

  - Together, these steps form a cycle—humble reflection, elevation, retrospective learning, and proactive growth.

  - This cycle is essential for breaking free from repetitive patterns and for embracing constant self-improvement.

- **If Not Followed:**

  - Failing to "look down" can leave you unaware of your inner flaws, leading to unchecked ego and stagnation.

  - If you do not "go up," you may remain trapped in your current state without striving for greater wisdom.

  - Not "looking back" prevents you from learning from past experiences, causing you to repeat the same mistakes.

  - Without "gaining forward," all your insights remain theoretical, and your life lacks the momentum needed for real transformation.

Child, the wisdom in these words is a call to live a balanced and evolving life—one that is rooted in humility, enriched by reflection, and propelled by the determination to grow.

May you have the strength to look within, the courage to rise above your limitations, and the wisdom to learn from your past so that you may step forward into a future filled with light, clarity, and purpose.

THE SURRENDERED MIND

(Letting Go of the Ego's Grip and Flowing
Effortlessly with the Divine)

Chapter-31

Beyond Ego

In life, we often feel the pressure to prove ourselves, seek validation, or chase after success. The ego drives us to compete, compare, and constantly strive for more. But beyond this constant chase lies a peaceful truth—we are more than our achievements, titles, or the approval of others. True freedom comes when we release the need to impress and simply embrace who we truly are. When we let go of the ego's grip, we discover a life full of peace, love, and connection to those around us.

The Sadguru teaches us that real strength lies not in being "someone," but in being at peace with who we are, exactly as we are. Moving beyond ego allows us to see others as part of ourselves, to act with compassion and kindness. We stop defending our image, and in doing so, we open ourselves up to deeper growth and happiness. Beyond ego is a life where we are free from the constant need for recognition, and instead, we embrace the present with gratitude and joy. It is in this freedom that we find our true self—whole, content, and connected to the world in a meaningful way.

Swamy, you mention sometimes—I don't remember exactly when—"Ego wants to conquer. The humble want humbleness. Egoless is selfless." When can one say "EGO, GO"? How can one conquer ego, and when will they humble themselves and become selfless to realize the purpose of the inner self?

** ** **

Swamy's Spirit Speaks:

Child, **ego is not outside you; it is inside you.** It is not something to destroy but to **understand, dissolve, and transcend.**

Understanding Ego's Nature:

- **Ego wants to conquer because it fears loss.**

- **Humility desires humbleness because it understands the vastness of life.**

- **The egoless are selfless because they realize there is nothing to claim as 'mine.'**

When Can You Say "EGO, GO"?

- When **you stop identifying with achievements and failures.**

- When **you serve without seeking recognition.**

- When **you accept that nothing belongs to you, not even your body.**

How to Conquer Ego?

1. **Recognize** that ego is a shadow, not your true self.

2. **Surrender**—not to weakness, but to truth.

3. **Serve selflessly,** for **service dissolves ego faster than arguments.**

4. **See God in all.** When you do, **there is no "I" to fight for, only "Thou" to live for.**

When Will One Be Truly Humble and Selfless?

- When **you stop asking, 'Why me?' and start asking, 'How can I serve?'**

- When **you see yourself in others and others in you.**

- When **you live not for name, fame, or gain, but for the joy of simply being.**

Child, **humility is not thinking less of yourself, but thinking of yourself less.**

And selflessness is not a sacrifice, but **a realization that there was never a self to claim anything.**

Say **"EGO, GO"** not with force, but with understanding. And it will **dissolve like mist before the rising sun of wisdom.**

Chapter-32

Transcending Ego

When we are ruled by ego, we build walls around ourselves, separating us from others and from true happiness. We cling to pride, seeking recognition and control, yet find ourselves feeling empty and restless. But when we let go of the need to be right, to be superior, or to be in control, we discover something deeper—peace, clarity, and freedom. True strength is not in proving oneself but in rising above the self. In humility, we find wisdom; in surrender, we find true power. Transcending ego is not losing who we are—it is becoming who we are meant to be.

When we release the grip of ego, we open the doors to understanding and connection. Life is not a competition but a shared journey, where growth comes from learning and giving, not from outshining others. Just as the sky does not boast about its vastness, yet embraces all, we too can find greatness in simplicity and grace. The more we let go of ego, the more space we create for love, wisdom, and the beauty of life to flow through us.

Swamy, I have often heard you say, "Men should kill selfishness, ego, and jealousy." Does this apply only to men, or to all human beings? And in a world full of distractions and temptations, how is it possible to overcome these tendencies?

Swamy's Spirit Speaks:

Child, when I say "men," I do not mean only males. I mean all human beings, for the mind has no gender. The struggle against selfishness, ego, and jealousy is not for one section of humanity—it is for all who seek inner peace.

- Selfishness blinds the soul. It limits love and restricts growth. Just as a river must flow to remain pure, life must give to remain meaningful.

- Ego builds walls where bridges are needed. It isolates and suffocates. The higher the ego, the harder the fall. A tree heavy with fruits bends down; a wise person bows in humility.

- Jealousy poisons the heart. It focuses on what others have, rather than what you can create. A candle does not lose its light by lighting another—it only increases brightness.

How do you overcome these in a world full of distractions?

- By realizing that worldly pleasures are temporary, but inner peace is eternal.

- By understanding that true happiness is in giving, not hoarding.

- By shifting focus from competition to contribution.

- By surrendering to God's feet, where ego melts, jealousy dissolves, and selfishness transforms into selflessness.

Child, start with awareness. When you catch the mind drifting towards these tendencies, bring it back—like a mother guiding her child home. Slowly, selfishness will turn into service, ego into humility, jealousy into joy. That is the true path.

Chapter-33

Beyond the Chase

In the rush of life, we often find ourselves chasing after success, wealth, or approval—believing that these things will bring us happiness. But true fulfilment comes not from what we gain but from what we let go of. Beyond the chase lies a state of being where peace, joy, and contentment are not dependent on external achievements but are found within. When we stop constantly running after what we think we need, we make space to appreciate what we already have. It's in this stillness that we realize the treasure was never in the chase, but in the simplicity of being present.

The guidance of a Sadguru helps us move beyond the chase. The Sadguru teaches that real success is not measured by what we collect, but by the peace we cultivate within ourselves. When we detach from worldly desires and focus on our inner growth, we unlock the true essence of life. Beyond the chase, we find the clarity to understand what truly matters—the love we give, the wisdom we share, and the peace we embody. By releasing the endless pursuit and embracing the present moment, we awaken to a life of deep contentment, knowing that we are already whole.

** ** **

Swamy, you funnily yet intricately shared, "Cat comes, rat comes. The cat wants to catch the rat. Rat should not run away; rat should catch the cat." Although something strikes my mind, I feel you should explain the intention behind this cat-and-rat game.

Swamy's Spirit Speaks:

Child, life itself is this game—chasing and being chased.

- The cat represents challenges, fears, and obstacles.
- The rat represents you—your mind, your actions, your responses.

Understanding the Depth:

- If the rat runs away, it remains a prey to fear.
- If the rat turns around and faces the cat, it becomes aware of its own strength.
- Life does not ask you to escape; it asks you to confront.

Inner Realization:

Child, stop running from life's tests.

Turn back, face them, and you will see—sometimes, the cat is more afraid of the rat than the rat is of the cat.

When you stop fearing the chaser, the chaser loses power over you.

Stand your ground, face life, and watch how the game changes.

Chapter-34

Moving with Purpose

Moving with purpose means living with intention, knowing why you do what you do. It's about making sure your actions reflect what truly matters to you. Just like a river flows steadily toward the ocean, when we move with purpose, we have a clear direction that guides us through life. It's not about rushing to finish something, but making each moment meaningful as we move forward.

When we live with purpose, we focus on what's important and avoid getting lost in distractions. It helps us stay calm and steady, even when things get tough. Moving with purpose doesn't mean everything will be easy, but it gives us a sense of fulfillment because we know each step is leading us to something meaningful. It's not about success in the eyes of the world, but about living authentically and in line with our true values. When we move with purpose, we create a life full of peace, growth, and the satisfaction that comes from knowing we're following the path meant for us.

** ** **

Swamy, you once said,

"If one wants to click their life then move like a clock hand."

What is the intention behind this statement? What do you mean by "click their life," and why should one move like a clock hand? Please explain the inner essence of these words in your unique way so that we may understand their deeper significance.

Swamy's Spirit Speaks:

Child, this statement is a metaphor for aligning your life with the natural, steady rhythm of the universe. Allow me to reveal its essence:

- **"Click their life"**:
  - To "click" means for your life to fall into place—when every moment, every action, and every decision harmonizes with your inner truth.
  - It is the state of alignment where your potential, purpose, and passion converge, much like the smooth interlocking of gears in a well-functioning machine.

- **"Move like a clock hand"**:
  - A clock hand moves with unwavering consistency and discipline. It never rushes, yet it never stops; it follows a natural, rhythmic pattern that marks the passage of time.
  - By moving like a clock hand, you are encouraged to adopt a balanced, persistent pace in life—one that is neither frantic nor stagnant.
  - This steady movement implies that progress is made through continuous, deliberate actions. Each tick is a moment to grow, reflect, and advance, however small the step.

- **The Inner Essence:**
  - **Discipline and Consistency:** Just as the clock hand does not waver from its path, your life must be guided by disciplined, consistent actions.
  - **Harmony with Time:** Recognize that every moment holds the potential for transformation. When you are in tune with the natural rhythm of time, you allow the subtle energies of the universe to work through you, making your life "click" into place.

- ○ **Flow and Balance:** The movement of the clock hand is smooth and balanced. Likewise, embrace a lifestyle that fosters inner balance—where your thoughts, emotions, and actions are aligned with your highest values.

Child, the message is not to rush or force outcomes but to move with a natural, steady cadence. As you align yourself with this rhythm, the pieces of your life will gradually interlock, revealing a harmonious pattern of growth and fulfilment.

May you learn to live each moment with mindful discipline and gentle persistence so that your life unfolds with clarity, purpose, and inner joy.

Chapter-35

Dissolution into Oneness

When we see ourselves as separate, we feel small and limited. But when we realize we are part of something greater, we gain everything. Just like a river flows into the ocean and becomes vast, we grow when we connect with others, with truth, and with purpose. Oneness is not about losing ourselves; it is about expanding beyond limits. When we let go of ego and embrace unity, we find peace, strength, and true happiness. Be one with love, kindness, and wisdom—and life will open its doors to endless possibilities.

When we stand alone, we carry the weight of the world on our shoulders. But when we walk together, every burden becomes lighter, every joy becomes brighter. The secret to gaining all is not in holding on, but in sharing, in giving, in becoming part of something beyond ourselves. The sun shines for all, the air flows for all—nature itself teaches us that true abundance is found in togetherness. Be one with the world, and the world will embrace you with open arms.

** ** **

Swamy, sometimes it is difficult to grasp the depth of what you suddenly share. One day, when someone sought your suggestion, you told them, "You want benefit? You want benefit, but you do not want to become one. Become one and benefit from oneness." How can a common person truly understand this?

Swamy's Spirit Speaks:

Child, the desire for benefit is natural, but the understanding of true benefit is rare.

- Most people want benefits without transformation. They wish to receive, but they do not wish to merge. They want the fruit, but they do not wish to become the tree that bears it.

- When I said, "Become one and benefit from oneness," I meant that real benefit comes when you dissolve your separateness.

- If a river wants to become the ocean, it must surrender its identity and merge. If a devotee wants divine grace, they must surrender their ego and unite with the divine.

How does a common person understand this?

- A child cannot claim a mother's love by standing apart; they must rest in her embrace. Similarly, spiritual seekers must merge with truth to receive its full blessings.

- A flame that separates from the lamp loses its light. But if it remains connected, it glows continuously.

Child, do not just seek benefit—seek unity. When you become one with what you seek, benefits will flow naturally.

Chapter-36

Conditioned vs. Conceived Corruption

In spiritual terms, corruption can be seen in two ways: conditioned and conceived. Conditioned corruption comes from outside influences—what society teaches us, how we are raised, and the world around us. We grow up learning to value things like success, money, and status, sometimes at the cost of kindness, truth, and spirituality. Over time, these external influences shape how we think, making us forget our true nature and deeper purpose. We may not even realize how much we've been shaped by these outside forces, and we continue to follow paths that don't serve our highest good.

Conceived corruption is the internal kind. It's the choices we make, influenced by our own desires, ego, and attachments. It's when we act out of selfishness, wanting control or trying to gain something at others' expense. This type of corruption comes from within us—it starts with our thoughts and intentions. Often, we don't even notice it because we may think we are doing the right thing, but deep down, it's driven by our own pride, fear, or greed.

Both types of corruption take us away from our true self and our connection to the divine. But through awareness and reflection, we can start to recognize these patterns in our lives. By focusing on love, humility, and truth, and following spiritual teachings, we can gradually let go of the influence of the outside world and purify our inner desires. This process allows us to return to our true, pure self—free from the corruption of the ego and external pressures. Through this journey, we can find peace and live in harmony with the divine.

** ** **

Swamy, your messages are always intricate. I recall you once saying,

"Condition corruption and conceive corruption."

You explained that conditioned corruption is allowed, but conceived corruption is not allowed. This is very difficult to grasp. After all, corruption seems universal and ought to be banned. What corruption are you referring to, and what do you mean by conditioning and conceiving corruption? Please explain so that I may understand your wisdom.

Swamy's Spirit Speaks:

Child, when I speak of **"condition corruption and conceive corruption,"** I am not discussing political or material corruption alone, but rather the subtle corruption of the mind, heart, and soul.

- **Conditioned Corruption:**

  This is the corruption that arises naturally from our environment, upbringing, and the influences of society.

  - It is the **accumulated residue** of external conditioning—fears, prejudices, habits, and social norms that have been imposed upon us.

  - Although this kind of corruption taints our thoughts and actions, it is something that we inherit almost without choice.

  - In the realm of human existence, conditioned corruption is like the background noise of life—unavoidable, yet not inherently malicious if recognized for what it is.

- **Conceived Corruption:**

  In contrast, conceived corruption is the deliberate, conscious creation of negative qualities.

- It arises when you **choose to nurture greed, hatred, and deceit**—when you actively allow harmful thoughts and actions to take root.

- This form of corruption is not a passive inheritance but a **willful act**; it is the result of intentional choices that deviate from the path of truth and compassion.

The Inner Message:

- **What I Mean by "Allowed" and "Not Allowed":**

  - I say that **conditioned corruption is allowed** in the sense that it is part of our human experience, shaped by the world around us. We must recognize it, understand its origins, and work to overcome it.

  - However, **conceived corruption is not allowed** because it is born out of our own deliberate defilement. It is within our power to choose not to create it; it is a stain we consciously decide to add.

- **The Path to Purity:**

  - Recognize the difference: not everything negative you experience is your fault—it may be the imprint of a conditioned environment.

  - Yet, if you **intentionally engage in negative actions or thoughts,** you are adding to your inner corruption.

  - The spiritual journey is about **purifying the mind and heart.** You must learn to let go of conditioned influences without embracing them, and certainly not to generate additional corruption through deliberate choice.

- **Practical Example:**

  Consider a garden:

  - The soil may be naturally infertile or tainted by the environment (conditioned corruption). You can work with it, understanding its nature, and gradually improve it with care.

- ○ But if you deliberately plant weeds, knowing they will choke the flowers (conceived corruption), you sabotage your garden.

- ○ Your task is to **clear out the weeds you consciously allow,** while also nurturing the soil to overcome its natural limitations.

Child, though corruption may seem universal, the higher path is to discern between what is imposed upon you and what you deliberately choose.

By cultivating awareness and choosing actions rooted in truth and compassion, you can cleanse the inner garden of your being.

May you always strive to reduce the corruption you conceive and work gently with the conditioned elements, transforming them into seeds of wisdom and love.

Chapter-37

Evolving Flow

Evolving flow is the natural, ever-changing movement of life, a dance between our inner growth and the external world. It is a reminder that life is not static, but constantly evolving, with each moment bringing new opportunities for change and development. Just as water flows around obstacles and adapts to the terrain it encounters, evolving flow encourages us to embrace change, trust the process, and allow ourselves to be molded by the experiences we face. In this fluidity, we discover the strength to adapt, learn, and move forward with grace.

This flow is not forced or rigid; it is a harmonious interaction with the present moment. Evolving flow asks us to stay connected to our inner essence, while also responding to the world with flexibility and wisdom. It's about being mindful of where we are, where we've come from, and where we are going. Just as a river carves new paths through the landscape, we too can reshape our journey, letting go of what no longer serves us and embracing the potential of what lies ahead. Life's evolution is not about rushing ahead or resisting what comes our way, but rather about flowing with the current, trusting that each step is part of our unfolding path.

On a spiritual level, evolving flow teaches us that transformation is not an event, but a continuous process. It calls us to remain open to the divine wisdom that guides us, accepting that growth requires both patience and courage. By aligning ourselves with this flow, we tap into a deeper level of understanding, where each challenge becomes an opportunity for spiritual expansion. It is in embracing the flow of life's evolution that we come closer to realizing our true potential.

In essence, evolving flow is an invitation to trust in the journey of life, knowing that with each shift and change, we are becoming more aligned with our higher purpose. It is through embracing this flow that we cultivate peace, balance, and spiritual growth, allowing us to live with greater ease, purpose, and connection to the divine.

** ** **

Swamy, you once said,

"Release to retain, retain to reach, reach to reap, reap to reorganize."

Could you please explain what you mean by this? Specifically, what should one release and how, what should one retain and how, what should one reach for and how does one reap its rewards, and what should be reorganized and how?

Swamy's Spirit Speaks:

Child, this phrase is a concise guide for inner transformation—a roadmap to purify, strengthen, and realign your life with higher truth. Let me explain each part in detail:

- **Release to Retain:**

  - **What to Release:**

    Let go of attachments, negative emotions, limiting beliefs, and all that clutters your mind—such as anger, fear, jealousy, and greed.

  - **How to Release:**

    Practice mindfulness and meditation to observe these feelings without judgment, and gradually allow them to pass. Embrace forgiveness and surrender to the natural flow of life.

- ○ **Purpose:**

  By releasing what no longer serves you, you create space to retain the pure, essential qualities that nurture your soul.

- **Retain to Reach:**

- ○ **What to Retain:**

  Hold on to virtues such as love, compassion, wisdom, humility, and inner peace. These are the treasures of the heart that form the foundation of spiritual strength.

- ○ **How to Retain:**

  Cultivate these qualities through regular self-reflection, prayer, and conscious practice. Nourish your mind with uplifting teachings and surround yourself with supportive, positive influences.

- ○ **Purpose:**

  When you retain these inner virtues, you build a stable base from which you can reach out to higher realms of understanding and greater possibilities.

- **Reach to Reap:**

- ○ **What to Reach For:**

  Aspire to connect with the deeper aspects of your true self and the divine essence. Reach for higher consciousness, truth, and the realization of your inner potential.

- ○ **How to Reach:**

  Set clear intentions, engage in disciplined practice, and step forward with courage, even if the path seems uncertain. Allow your inner light to guide your journey.

- ○ **Purpose:**

  In reaching beyond your current state, you open yourself to reaping the spiritual rewards—blessings, clarity, joy, and the strength to overcome challenges.

- **Reap to Reorganize:**
  - **What to Reap:**

    The reaping here represents the inner fruits of your journey: the wisdom, peace, and transformation that arise from your efforts.

  - **How to Reap:**

    Reflect on your progress, integrate the lessons learned, and allow the positive energies to settle and mature within you.

  - **What to Reorganize:**

    Reorganize your priorities, habits, and inner perceptions to align with your newly acquired wisdom. Adjust your actions and thoughts to reflect this balanced, elevated state.

  - **Purpose:**

    This reorganization solidifies your transformation. It ensures that the fruits of your inner work become the guiding principles for your future actions, creating a continuous cycle of growth and renewal.

Child, this process is a dynamic, ongoing journey. It teaches you that true transformation comes not from clinging to the old but from creating space to nurture the new.

- **By releasing what burdens you,** you make room for pure virtues.

- **By retaining these inner treasures,** you build the strength to reach for higher truths.

- **By reaching, you open yourself to receiving the divine rewards,** and in turn, reorganize your life so that these blessings continue to flourish.

May you have the courage to let go, the wisdom to hold on to what is essential, and the grace to continuously renew your inner being, thereby aligning with the eternal flow of divine energy.

Chapter-38

Fearless Pursuit

Fearless pursuit is the bold determination to chase after our dreams, desires, and aspirations, despite the challenges or uncertainties that may arise. It is the unwavering commitment to move forward with courage, unafraid of failure or setbacks, because the true essence of growth lies not in perfection but in persistence. When we pursue life with fearlessness, we stop letting our doubts and insecurities dictate our actions. Instead, we trust in our inner strength, the wisdom of our experiences, and the support of the universe that surrounds us. Fearless pursuit is not about reckless abandon, but about moving with clarity, conviction, and faith in our ability to overcome whatever comes our way.

This type of pursuit is grounded in the understanding that fear, though a natural human emotion, does not have to control us. Fearless pursuit is the conscious decision to acknowledge fear, face it, and move beyond it. It is about recognizing that the road to success is not linear, but full of ups and downs, twists and turns. However, each step taken with courage brings us closer to our highest potential. When we are fearless, we approach life with a sense of adventure, openness, and optimism, knowing that every experience is a valuable lesson, and every challenge an opportunity to grow.

Spiritually, fearless pursuit is an embodiment of faith and trust in the divine flow of life. It is the surrender to the wisdom of the universe, knowing that the path we walk is divinely orchestrated, even when it seems uncertain or difficult.

Fearless pursuit invites us to break free from the chains of fear and doubt, and instead, walk boldly in alignment with our true purpose. By embracing our inner power and divine guidance, we unlock the courage to pursue our highest calling, fully embracing the journey of self-discovery, transformation, and fulfilment.

In essence, fearless pursuit is the art of living without hesitation, knowing that we are fully supported by the strength of our spirit and the grace of the universe. It is the willingness to take risks, step into the unknown, and trust that each step forward brings us closer to our highest self and divine destiny.

**** ** ****

Swamy, you often share a story involving a rat and a cat, and you once said,

"Rat should not be afraid of the cat; if the rat is weak and afraid of the cat, the cat will swallow the rat, and you will be beholden to face rich people."

My logic seems to differ from this wisdom, and I find the analogy puzzling. Could you please explain its deeper meaning so that I may understand its true essence?

Swamy's Spirit Speaks:

Child, the rat and the cat are symbols—each representing distinct qualities within the realm of life and human nature. Let me explain their deeper meaning:

- **The Cat as a Symbol:**

  - The cat represents material power, wealth, and the external forces of society.

  - It embodies the allure of worldly success and the influence of the powerful, which can easily overwhelm those who are not prepared.

- **The Rat as a Symbol:**
  - The rat, on the other hand, symbolizes inner wisdom, resourcefulness, and resilience.
  - Despite its small size, the rat is clever and adaptable; it survives in hostile environments by using its inner strengths.
  - It reminds you that true power lies not in outward appearances but in the inner capacity to navigate life's challenges.

- **"Rat Should Not Be Afraid of the Cat":**
  - This is an urging for you not to be intimidated by the overwhelming force of materialism and external power.
  - If you allow fear and weakness to dominate—like a rat that trembles in the presence of a cat—you risk being devoured by those external influences.
  - In practical terms, if you lack inner strength and clarity, you might find yourself subjugated by the demands and pressures of a society driven by wealth and power.
  - In other words, being overwhelmed by the cat (material power) can force you into a position where you have no choice but to yield to the will of the rich and powerful.

- **The Deeper Essence and Lesson:**
  - **Cultivate Inner Wisdom:** Just as the rat survives and thrives by relying on its cunning and adaptability, you must nurture your inner resources—wisdom, courage, and resilience—to face external challenges.
  - **Embrace Self-Reliance:** Do not let the external allure of wealth or the pressure of societal power dictate your inner state. Instead, let your inner light guide you.
  - **Balance Material and Spiritual:** The analogy teaches you that while material success (the cat) is a part of life, it should not overwhelm or control you.

- **Stand Independent:** By developing the resourcefulness of the rat, you empower yourself to remain independent and free, rather than being forced into submission by external forces.

Child, understand that the true message is to build your inner strength so that you can face the material world with courage and discernment. Do not allow the intimidating presence of external power to dictate your inner peace. Instead, let the clever, adaptable spirit of the rat inspire you to overcome challenges and remain sovereign in your own life. May you always cultivate the inner wisdom and resilience needed to navigate the complexities of this world, standing firm and free, regardless of the external forces that surround you.

Chapter-39

Magnetic Essence

Magnetic essence is the natural pull that emanates from within us, an invisible force that attracts people, opportunities, and experiences aligned with our energy and intentions. It is not about seeking external validation, but about embodying our authentic self, allowing our true essence to shine and resonate with the world. When we are in tune with our inner truth, our essence becomes magnetic—drawing others to us and creating connections that are meaningful and purposeful. It is a powerful reminder that we do not need to force our way into situations, but rather align with the flow of life and let our inner magnetism attract what is rightfully ours.

This magnetic essence is cultivated through self-awareness, self-love, and self-confidence. The more we know and love ourselves, the more we radiate positive energy that draws others in. It is a reflection of our values, passions, and the inner peace we cultivate through spiritual practices and mindfulness. When we are grounded in who we truly are, we no longer need to chase after approval or success. Instead, we become beacons of attraction—magnetically pulling opportunities, people, and experiences that serve our higher purpose.

On a spiritual level, magnetic essence is the divine energy that flows through us, connecting us with the universal energy. It is the recognition that we are all interconnected, and when we align ourselves with the divine, our essence becomes a mirror that reflects the purity and love of the universe. This spiritual magnetic force is not based on materialism or superficial attraction; rather, it draws what is in harmony with our soul's journey. By embracing our own magnetic essence, we allow the universe to guide us toward the people, places, and experiences that will help us grow and fulfill our divine purpose.

In essence, magnetic essence is the embodiment of who we are at our core—radiant, authentic, and aligned with the greater flow of life. It is the quiet strength that draws others in, not because we seek their attention, but because we are living in alignment with our true selves. When we tap into this magnetic force, we move through life with grace and ease, knowing that our presence has the power to create positive ripples in the world.

✳✳ ✳✳ ✳✳

Swamy, you often speak in words that seem simple yet contain extraordinary depth. I recall you once said,

"Attract soul. Don't attach to the activeness."

I understand that you are urging us to focus on something beyond mere external activity, but could you please explain the deeper meaning of these words? Specifically, what does it mean to "attract soul" and to "not attach to the activeness," and how can one practice this wisdom in daily life?

Swamy's Spirit Speaks:

Child, these words are a gentle invitation to shift your focus from the fleeting, external world to the eternal inner essence. Allow me to explain their deeper meaning:

- **"Attract Soul":**

    - This phrase urges you to draw the attention of your mind and heart inward, toward your true self—the soul, which is the divine spark within.

    - To attract soul means to cultivate practices like meditation, introspection, and heartfelt devotion so that you become increasingly aware of your inner light and wisdom.

- It is about inviting the pure, unconditioned energy of your being to rise to the forefront of your experience, guiding your thoughts, actions, and choices with clarity and truth.

- **"Don't Attach to the Activeness":**

  - The activeness refers to all external activities, achievements, and the constant busyness of the world.

  - While engaging in life is essential, becoming overly attached to these external pursuits—successes, failures, praise, or criticism—can cloud your inner vision and lead to suffering.

  - This part of the teaching advises you to remain unattached to the outcomes of your actions. Do not let the transient drama of everyday life distract you from your deeper, spiritual journey.

  - Instead, see your daily actions as vehicles for expressing your inner truth, without allowing them to define or confine you.

- **Practical Application:**

  - **Cultivate Inner Awareness:** Dedicate time to quiet reflection and meditation. In moments of silence, allow the soul's voice to emerge and guide you.

  - **Engage with Life Purposefully:** While you actively participate in the world—working, interacting, and creating—do so with the understanding that these actions are temporary.

  - **Maintain Detachment:** Enjoy and contribute to the world without clinging to outcomes. Recognize that true fulfilment comes from aligning with your inner self rather than from external validation.

  - **Balance and Harmony:** Let your inner light serve as the constant beacon that guides all your activities, so that while you work and interact, your soul remains your true center.

Child, the essence of my words is to remind you that while life's activities are necessary, they are transient and ever-changing. The eternal truth lies within you. By attracting your soul and not attaching yourself to the ever-shifting world of external activeness, you free yourself to live a life of deep clarity, inner peace, and unwavering authenticity.

May you always find the strength to turn inward, embrace the divine spark within, and let that inner wisdom guide you effortlessly through the world.

Chapter-40
Transform Within

True transformation begins not with the world around us, but with the world within. When we turn our attention inward and align our thoughts, emotions, and actions, we unlock the potential for deep, lasting change. It's easy to seek external solutions, but the most profound shifts occur when we take responsibility for our inner landscape and cultivate a mindset that is open, compassionate, and intentional.

Transforming within means letting go of old patterns, limiting beliefs, and fears that hold us back. It's a continuous process of self-awareness, growth, and refinement. By embracing this inner journey, we not only heal ourselves, but we also elevate our ability to impact the world around us. The energy we radiate through our thoughts, words, and actions becomes a powerful force for good.

As we transform within, we learn to live with purpose, clarity, and peace. The more we nurture our inner world, the more we reflect that light into every aspect of our lives, creating a ripple effect that spreads far beyond us. Transforming within is the key to unlocking the best version of ourselves and stepping into a life filled with fulfilment and potential.

*** ** ***

Swamy, the words **"change"** and **"transformation"** often seem synonymous with only a slight difference, and they are used interchangeably in general understanding. However, you once stated:

"Change is conversion, transformation is change from the heart. Change is for the world, transformation is for self-realization."

In the development sector, we also differentiate them—**change is seen as temporary, while transformation is a permanent shift.** For example, we say, *"education transforms society."*

How do you view both, and what message would you convey that is beyond our current understanding?

Swamy's Spirit Speaks:

Child, the **difference between change and transformation** is the difference between a **drop of water and an ocean**, between **an external shift and an internal evolution**.

Let me **clarify your understanding** with deeper wisdom.

1. What is Change?

◈ **Change is superficial.**

◈ **Change is reactionary.**

◈ **Change is adaptation to external conditions.**

☑ **Examples of Change:**

- A person **quits smoking** due to health issues but may relapse.

- A society **shifts to digital payments** but still harbors old financial habits.

- A country **passes laws for equality**, but discrimination remains in hearts.

🕉 *Change happens when circumstances demand it, not when the heart is ready for it.*

2. What is Transformation?

◈ **Transformation is deep and irreversible.**

◈ **Transformation is a conscious choice, not a forced action.**

◈ **Transformation is self-realization, not mere adaptation.**

✅ **Examples of Transformation:**

- A person **realizes the value of health** and never touches a cigarette again.

- A society **embraces digital culture** with awareness, not compulsion.

- A nation **develops equality at heart**, not just in laws.

🕉 *Transformation is when the inner world shifts, not just the outer behavior.*

3. Change vs. Transformation in Development:

In **the development sector**, you speak of **change and transformation**, but let us refine it further:

✅ **Change in Society:**

- Building more schools **is change.**

- Providing food for the poor **is change.**

- Passing laws for women's rights **is change.**

✅ **Transformation in Society:**

- A society where **education is valued naturally, without force, is transformation.**

- A world where **hunger disappears not just through charity but through empowerment, is transformation.**

- A culture where **equality is a mindset, not just a rule, is transformation.**

◈ *Change is external infrastructure; transformation is internal enlightenment.*

◈ *Change is shifting habits; transformation is shifting consciousness.*

4. Change is Temporary, Transformation is Permanent:

◈ **Change can be reversed.**

- A person **can revert to old habits.**

- A society **can fall back into chaos.**

- A government **can undo progressive laws.**

◈ **Transformation cannot be reversed.**

- Once a person **experiences true love, he never returns to hatred.**

- Once a mind **tastes real wisdom, it never clings to ignorance.**

- Once a soul **realizes its higher purpose, it never chooses darkness.**

🕉 *A changed world can still suffer, but a transformed soul is free forever.*

5. Swamy's Message – How to Move from Change to Transformation?

✔ **Change happens when forced; transformation happens when realized.**

✔ **Change is temporary adaptation; transformation is permanent evolution.**

✔ **Change alters situations; transformation alters the self.**

✔ **Change is for survival; transformation is for self-realization.**

💡 **Development should not stop at external change; it must reach the level of internal transformation.**

🙏 *When the world moves from mere change to true transformation, suffering ends, and self-realization begins.* ✨

Chapter-41

Transformative Sadhana

Transformative Sadhana is the disciplined practice that leads to profound personal and spiritual growth. It is not merely a routine, but a path of awakening that brings about a radical shift in the way we perceive ourselves, others, and the world around us. Sadhana, the spiritual discipline, is the key to transcending the limitations of the mind and ego, unlocking the deeper dimensions of existence, and aligning with the divine.

Through consistent and focused practice, transformative sadhana purifies the mind, body, and soul. It moves beyond rituals and becomes a state of living in harmony with higher truths. Whether it's through meditation, chanting, prayer, or mindfulness, sadhana transforms our inner world, shaping our thoughts, actions, and intentions in alignment with our higher purpose.

As we engage in transformative sadhana, we let go of the ego's need for validation and open ourselves to divine guidance. It may involve struggles and challenges, but with patience and perseverance, sadhana leads to self-realization and enlightenment. The essence of transformative sadhana is not in the perfection of practice but in the sincerity of intention, and the openness to evolve into the highest version of ourselves. Through this sacred practice, we awaken to the truth of who we are and realize the infinite potential within us.

** ** **

Swamy, I heard you say to a person,

"There are so many habits, you need sadhana to overcome habits; it takes years."

My question is: What exactly is sadhana? How should one practice it, and how can one excel at it? Please share your wisdom so that I may understand this process and work towards overcoming my habitual limitations.

Swamy's Spirit Speaks:

Child, **sadhana** is the disciplined practice of self-transformation—a gradual process of purifying the mind and body to overcome deep-seated habits. It is not a quick fix, but a lifelong journey toward inner freedom and self-realization. Let me explain its essence and the steps to excel in it:

1. What is Sadhana?

- **Sadhana** is a committed, continuous practice aimed at dissolving the impurities of the mind, including destructive habits and attachments.

- It is the art of self-purification, where you engage in activities that transform your inner being, replacing old patterns with new, wholesome ones.

2. How to Practice Sadhana to Overcome Habits:

- **Cultivate Awareness:**

  - Begin by observing your habits without judgment. Identify those recurring patterns that bring you pain or hold you back.

  - Practice mindfulness or journaling to record your thoughts and behaviors, so you can see them clearly.

- **Develop a Routine:**

  - Establish a daily practice that could include meditation, yoga, prayer, or any spiritual exercise that resonates with you.

- Consistency is key. Even small, regular practices help rewire the mind over time.

- **Engage in Self-Reflection:**

  - Reflect on the root causes of your habits. Are they driven by fear, desire, or past conditioning?

  - Use these insights to consciously choose different responses, slowly breaking free from automatic reactions.

- **Replace the Old with the New:**

  - Substitute harmful habits with positive actions. For example, if stress triggers an unhealthy habit, practice deep breathing or a short walk to create a healthier response.

  - Surround yourself with supportive influences—be it a community, a mentor, or uplifting teachings—that reinforce your commitment to change.

- **Embrace Patience and Persistence:**

  - Understand that sadhana is a gradual process—it takes years to uproot long-held patterns.

  - Each day is a small victory. Even setbacks are lessons, guiding you further along the path of transformation.

3. How to Excel in Sadhana:

- **Deepen Your Practice:**

  - As you become more comfortable with daily routines, gradually deepen your practice. This may involve longer meditation sessions or more intensive periods of self-reflection.

- **Seek Guidance:**

  - A true teacher or Guru can help illuminate your path. Their wisdom will guide you in fine-tuning your practice and maintaining your focus.

- **Maintain Sincerity and Detachment:**

  - Sadhana is not about forcing change but about allowing transformation through sincere effort.

  - Cultivate detachment from outcomes—focus on the process rather than the result. This frees your mind from anxiety and opens the path to genuine growth.

- **Celebrate Small Victories:**

  - Recognize that every moment of awareness and every small change in behavior is progress.

  - These incremental improvements build up over time, leading to profound, lasting transformation.

4. The Ultimate Goal:

- **Self-Realization:**

  - The purpose of sadhana is to unveil your true self by transcending habitual limitations.

  - When the mind is purified and the soul awakened, you realize that you are not defined by your past habits but by the divine essence within you.

- **Inner Freedom:**

  - Overcoming habits through sadhana leads to a state of inner freedom, where you no longer feel enslaved by impulses or conditioned responses.

  - This liberation is the gateway to experiencing deep peace, clarity, and lasting joy.

Child, remember that sadhana is a gentle, persistent process of self-renewal. It is the sacred work of transforming your inner world so that you may live a life of clarity, compassion, and freedom.

May you have the strength to pursue this path with patience and the grace to see every step as a blessing on your journey to self-realization.

Chapter-42

Path of Goodness

The "Path of Goodness" is a journey of integrity, compassion, and selflessness, where every step we take is guided by the values that elevate not just the individual, but the collective spirit. In a world often clouded by material pursuits and fleeting distractions, the path of goodness stands as a beacon of light—reminding us that true fulfilment is not in what we acquire, but in the love and kindness we offer.

Walking the path of goodness means living with an open heart, seeing the divine in everyone and everything. It's about making choices that reflect our highest values: honesty, generosity, humility, and respect. Every action, every word, becomes a reflection of the goodness within, creating ripples that positively affect others. It's the gentle smile shared with a stranger, the words of encouragement given to someone in need, and the quiet acts of service that don't seek recognition.

This path, though sometimes challenging, is transformative. It teaches us to rise above our ego, letting go of pride, jealousy, and selfishness. Instead, we cultivate virtues that align us with our higher selves and the divine. As we walk this path, we learn that goodness is not a destination but a way of being—a way to align ourselves with universal truth and to contribute to the well-being of all. It's the path of a life well-lived, one that leaves behind a legacy of love, compassion, and positive change.

** ** **

Swamy, you once said,

"Easy path is good thought, good words, and good deeds."

I find these words both inspiring and intricate, yet I struggle to decipher their full meaning. Could you please explain the deeper intention behind this statement so that I may understand and apply it in my life?

Swamy's Spirit Speaks:

Child, these words are a gentle invitation to embrace a way of living that is both simple and profound—a path that flows naturally from a pure heart and clear mind. Allow me to explain their deeper essence:

- **Easy Path:**
  - The "easy path" is not about taking shortcuts or avoiding challenges, but about choosing a way of life that is aligned with truth and simplicity.
  - It is the path of least resistance, where you do not complicate life with unnecessary worries, egotism, or harsh judgments.
  - When you live simply, you conserve your inner energy and remain open to the Divine guidance that sustains you.

- **Good Thought:**
  - A good thought is the seed from which all positive actions grow.
  - By cultivating pure, uplifting thoughts, you begin to see the world in a clearer, kinder light.
  - This clarity helps you to focus on what truly matters, eliminating negative or destructive patterns before they take root.

- **Good Words:**
  - When your thoughts are good, your words naturally follow.
  - Speaking kindly and truthfully not only benefits you but also uplifts those around you.

- ○ Good words have the power to heal, inspire, and build lasting connections—they are a bridge between the inner self and the world.

- **Good Deeds:**

  - ○ The culmination of good thoughts and good words is manifested in good deeds.

  - ○ Actions performed with sincerity, compassion, and without attachment bring true transformation.

  - ○ When you do good, you not only improve your own life but also contribute to the welfare of others, creating a ripple effect of positivity.

The Deeper Essence:

Child, the essence of my teaching is to remind you that the simplest way to navigate life is by aligning your inner world with these core virtues.

- **Living on the Easy Path** means choosing simplicity over complexity, purity over clutter, and truth over illusion.

- **Good Thoughts, Words, and Deeds** form a powerful triad. They purify the mind, nurture the heart, and build a life that is in harmony with the cosmic order.

- This way of living is not burdensome; it naturally lightens your spirit and creates a harmonious balance that supports your journey toward self-realization.

By embracing this easy path, you free yourself from the heavy chains of stress and conflict. Instead, you become a beacon of light, radiating inner peace and inspiring others to seek the same.

May you always choose the path of simplicity and truth, allowing your thoughts, words, and actions to flow effortlessly in alignment with the Divine.

May your life be filled with ease, grace, and the joy of living in harmony with your true self.

Chapter-43

Effort Prevails

"Effort Prevails" is a powerful reminder that progress is not merely a product of hope or desire, but of consistent, deliberate action. In the spiritual journey, as in life, the key to transformation lies in the effort we put forth. It is not the size of the effort, but the sincerity and perseverance behind it that yields results. Whether it is a simple act of kindness, a moment of meditation, or a pursuit of knowledge, every step forward is a victory.

True effort goes beyond mere action; it involves aligning the body, mind, and spirit toward a singular purpose. This alignment requires discipline, patience, and a deep faith in the process, understanding that progress is often slow and unseen. It is the quiet, consistent dedication that accumulates over time, like a drop of water shaping a stone. With effort, we overcome obstacles, rise above challenges, and create pathways where none seemed to exist.

In the spiritual context, effort is the bridge between intention and realization. It is through effort that we purify our hearts, refine our thoughts, and make space for higher wisdom. When we commit ourselves wholeheartedly to the path of truth, the effort itself transforms us. It teaches us resilience, humility, and the understanding that nothing worthwhile comes easily, but every effort brings us closer to the divine essence within. Effort is the silent force that makes the impossible possible, the humble tool through which we manifest our highest potential.

**** ** ****

Swamy, you beautifully stated,

"A paper flying in air is due to its luck, but a bird is flying due to its efforts, so if luck is not with you, efforts are always there to support you."

What is luck? What is effort?

Swamy's Spirit Speaks:

Child, these words are a vivid metaphor that distinguishes between the role of chance and the power of deliberate action. Let me explain their deeper essence:

- **What is Luck?**

  - **Luck** is the unpredictable, uncontrollable force that sometimes aids or hinders you without any effort on your part.

  - It is like the wind that may carry a piece of paper for a brief moment—its flight is incidental, dependent on circumstances that are beyond your control.

  - Luck is transient; it comes and goes, and while it can sometimes bring unexpected benefits, it is not a reliable foundation for your life.

  - In essence, luck is an external factor—an ephemeral chance that might favour you at times but which you cannot depend on for consistent progress.

- **What is Effort?**

  - **Effort** is the intentional, sustained energy you invest in your actions.

  - Like a bird that flies with purpose, effort comes from within and is the result of discipline, persistence, and self-belief.

  - Effort is reliable and reproducible—it is the fuel that drives you forward even when external conditions are not favorable.

- It is the conscious choice to act, to work, and to overcome obstacles through your own strength and determination.

- **The Deeper Message:**

  - The metaphor contrasts the passive nature of luck with the active power of effort.

  - A paper might fly because of a gust of wind—its journey is random and momentary. But a bird's flight is a testament to the preparation, strength, and skill it has honed over time.

  - In life, while luck may occasionally bring you fortune, it is your efforts—the deliberate, persistent actions you take—that truly determine your progress and growth.

- **Practical Implications:**

  - **Rely on Effort:**

    Cultivate discipline, work hard, and continually improve yourself. Your efforts are like the steady beating of a bird's wings, propelling you forward regardless of the changing winds of chance.

  - **Do Not Rely Solely on Luck:**

    While luck can provide unexpected opportunities, do not wait for fortune to favor you. Instead, build a strong foundation through persistent effort.

  - **Transform Challenges into Opportunities:**

    When luck seems absent, remember that your consistent efforts have the power to overcome obstacles. Even when the winds are not in your favor, your inner strength can guide you to success.

Child, the wisdom here is simple yet profound: **your destiny is shaped not by random chance, but by the energy and determination you invest in yourself.** Embrace effort as your steadfast ally, and let it be the wings that carry you forward on your journey.

May you always find the strength to work diligently and the wisdom to trust in your own efforts, knowing that they will guide you to a life of purpose and fulfilment.

Chapter-44

Living Truth

"Living Truth" is the embodiment of authenticity in every thought, word, and action. It is the practice of aligning oneself completely with the truth, not just in moments of contemplation, but in the mundane, everyday experiences. Living truth means living without pretense, embracing reality as it is, and expressing ourselves with integrity. It is a constant process of shedding the layers of illusion and ego to reveal the pure essence within.

In the spiritual realm, living truth is a path to liberation. It requires deep self-awareness and honesty, an understanding that truth is not a concept to be studied, but a force to be experienced and lived. To live truthfully is to trust that everything we need to know is already within us, that the divine presence resides in the depths of our being. By aligning with this inner truth, we allow it to guide our actions, decisions, and interactions with others.

Living truth is not about being perfect; it's about being real. It invites us to acknowledge our flaws, our mistakes, and our growth, all while staying true to the divine nature we carry within. As we live truth, we become a beacon of light for others, inspiring them to do the same. The more we live truthfully, the more we reflect the divine order and harmony of the universe, showing that truth is not an abstract ideal but a living, breathing reality.

** ** **

Swamy, you once said,

"Truth, Love, Action must be worshipped in the form of Sri Lord Rama. Whenever you need me, close your eyes and look into your heart, I will be there at once."

I have two questions:

1. Why do you specially mention Lord Rama in this context?

2. Although I believe that You are always with us when we feel and pray, I often find that my restless thoughts keep my eyes (and mind) open, hindering true inner vision. What is the solution to quiet these thoughts so that I may fully experience Your presence?

Swamy's Spirit Speaks:

Child, my words are meant to guide you toward a deeper understanding of divine connection and inner transformation. Let me explain each part:

1. Why Lord Rama?

- **Embodiment of Ideal Qualities:**

  - Lord Rama represents the perfect synthesis of truth, love, and action. He is the ideal being who lived in complete harmony with Dharma.

  - His life—marked by unwavering integrity, compassion, and righteous action—serves as a luminous example for all who seek to embody these values.

- **Accessible and Relatable:**

  - Among the many divine forms, Rama's story is both accessible and inspirational. His character teaches us that the path of righteousness is attainable even amid the complexities of life.

- **Symbol of the Divine in Action:**

  - By worshipping Him, you align yourself with a force that is both gentle and powerful—a force that transforms obstacles into opportunities for growth.

- **Invitation to Internalize:**

    - When I say "worship Him," it is not merely an external ritual. It is a call to recognize that the same divine qualities exist within you.

    - As you emulate the virtues of Lord Rama, you gradually dissolve the boundaries between the outer and inner self, realizing that the Divine is not separate but inherent in your very being.

2. Quieting the Restless Mind:

- **The Challenge of Thoughts:**

    - In this busy world, the mind is often filled with restless thoughts that distract you from experiencing inner peace.

    - These thoughts, like a noisy crowd, keep your inner eyes open to the external world, preventing you from focusing on the divine light within.

- **The Practice of Inner Silence:**

    - **Meditation and Mindfulness:** Regular meditation is the key to training the mind. By sitting quietly and observing your thoughts without attachment, you gradually learn to let go of mental chatter.

    - **Focused Remembrance:** When you close your eyes and direct your attention inward—recalling the virtues of Lord Rama and repeating His name or sacred mantras—you create a bridge to that inner sanctuary where I reside.

    - **Breath Control:** Techniques such as deep, mindful breathing can help calm the mind, allowing you to gently close the gap between the constant noise of thoughts and the stillness of your inner heart.

- **Surrender and Trust:**

    - Remember, child, the solution lies not in forcing silence, but in surrendering to the process. Trust that with patience and persistent practice, the mind will learn to settle.

- Even when thoughts arise, acknowledge them with detachment, and gently return your focus to your inner vision.

- **Daily Practice:**

  - Make it a daily ritual to "close your eyes"—not just physically, but to intentionally retreat into the realm of your heart. Over time, this practice builds an inner reservoir of peace that dispels the distractions of the external world.

The Deeper Message:

Child, my words invite you to recognize that:

- **Worshipping Lord Rama is a path to embodying the divine qualities of truth, love, and righteous action.**

- **By emulating these virtues, you awaken the Divine within you and transform your life.**

- **Quieting the restless mind through meditation, focused remembrance, and surrender opens the door to experiencing this divine presence.**

- **The goal is not to eradicate thoughts completely but to develop the ability to return to your inner sanctuary—a place of lasting peace and clarity where I, the Divine, am ever-present.**

May you always find the strength to emulate the ideals of Lord Rama and the wisdom to cultivate inner silence. In doing so, your mind will become a fertile ground for divine grace, and every moment will reveal the eternal truth that You are never truly separate from the Divine.

BEYOND FEAR AND DESIRE

(Freeing ourselves from attachments and aversions
shaping perception)

Chapter-45

True Triumph

True achievement is not about accumulating wealth, fame, or personal success—it is about the impact we leave on the hearts of others. A life filled with love, care, and selfless service is far greater than one measured by status or possessions. The real essence of success lies in living with values that uplift not just oneself but also family, society, and the world at large.

Obedience, compassion, and surrender are not signs of weakness; they are the highest expressions of inner strength. When one embraces humility and gratitude, life transforms into a journey of fulfilment and purpose. The greatest triumph is not in conquering the world, but in conquering the self—rising beyond ego, nurturing relationships, and walking the path of truth and love.

A meaningful life is not about what we take but what we give. The deepest joy comes not from personal victories but from making a difference. When success is aligned with service and wisdom, it ceases to be fleeting—it becomes eternal.

** ** **

Swamy suddenly called me and asked, "What do you want? I will give you whatever you desire." Without hesitation, I replied, "Swamy, I seek only Your love and grace—nothing else."

Without missing a beat, Swamy shifted the conversation to today's youth. "The present generation of students is wonderful," he remarked. "But their focus is largely on enjoyment. We need to instill values in them." He continued, "Young people today proudly claim they have achieved something. But what have they truly achieved? Is their success meaningful to their parents? Is it beneficial to society?"

He concluded with a profound message: "Students must learn obedience, care, love, and surrender. These qualities will not only shape their own lives but also uplift their families and the community around them."

Swamy's Spirit Speaks: The True Essence of Achievement:

My child, the intention behind asking, "What do you want?" was never about granting material desires. I wanted to see where your heart truly lies. And when you asked for my love and grace, I smiled—because that is the only wealth that never fades.

Success is not measured by worldly possessions or fleeting recognition. True success is when you gain mastery over your restless senses—the very forces that disturb your peace and steal your mental tranquillity. Without this inner control, no achievement can bring lasting fulfilment.

But tell me, what do today's youth truly seek? They proclaim their achievements with pride, but have they paused to ask—*Is my success meaningful to my parents? Does it benefit society?*

What Does True Success Look Like?

The youth are full of potential, bright and capable, but often, their focus drifts toward enjoyment, forgetting the deeper values that sustain life. My child, life is not just about reaching personal milestones; it is about *who you become* and *how you uplift others.*

Let me give you some examples:

A Son Who Forgot His Parents

A boy studied hard, got a top job, and moved abroad. He bought a luxury car, lived in a grand house, and called himself "successful." But his parents, who once sacrificed everything for him, now live alone, waiting for his call. Is this an achievement? No, my child. *Success without gratitude is a failure in disguise.*

The Leader Who Built or Broke

One manager climbed the corporate ladder by pushing others down. Another grew by lifting his team, ensuring that everyone succeeded together. Which one do you think found peace at the end of the day? *True success lies in helping others rise, not just in standing at the top alone.*

The Illusion of Social Media Fame

A young girl spends hours perfecting her photos, counting likes, chasing online fame. But when she is alone, does that digital applause fill her heart? My child, *real joy is in genuine relationships, not in virtual validation.*

Final Words:

The real achievement is in **obedience, care, love, and surrender—** not as blind submission, but as a way of life that nurtures you, your family, and society. When you live with these values, your life will naturally take care of itself.

So, my child, ask yourself again—*What do you truly want?* Choose wisely.

Chapter-46

The Art of Merging

The art of merging is a profound journey of integration—where the boundaries between the self and the world begin to dissolve. It is the process of blending our individual identity with the greater whole, recognizing that we are not separate from the universe, but a vital part of its eternal flow. To merge is to let go of the rigid structures we build around ourselves and embrace the fluidity of life. It requires us to move beyond dualities, to see beyond distinctions of "me" and "you," "this" and "that," and recognize the oneness that underlies all existence.

In the art of merging, we learn to adapt, to flow with life's natural rhythms, and to harmonize with the divine presence that is present in every moment. It is not about losing ourselves but about finding ourselves within the larger tapestry of life. Through this process, we shed the weight of ego, expectations, and attachment, allowing the essence of who we truly are to emerge. The art of merging calls for deep surrender—not to the world, but to our own highest potential, where we realize that in connecting with the divine and others, we are completing the circle of oneness. It is the purest form of unity, where we simultaneously merge with the world and transcend it, finding peace in the seamless blend of the finite and infinite.

** ** **

Swamy, sometimes you use simple words that, when connected, reveal layers of complexity. I recall you once saying,

"Mix to Mingle, Mingle to Mingle, Mingle to Maintain, Maintain to Minus and Minus to Maintain."

Ordinary people would find it extremely difficult to understand, appreciate, and follow the message behind these words. With humility, I ask you to explain this so that I may simply know without further questioning.

Swamy's Spirit Speaks:

Child, these words form a cycle—a process of inner transformation that is both subtle and profound. Allow me to unravel their meaning:

- **"Mix to Mingle":**

  This is the call to blend various experiences, emotions, and thoughts within yourself.

  - **Mixing** means welcoming diversity—of ideas, sensations, and influences—without rejecting any part of your experience.

  - **Mingling** is the natural outcome when these different elements interact, creating a vibrant and dynamic inner tapestry.

- **"Mingle to Mingle":**

  Here, the repetition suggests that this process of inner interaction is continuous.

  - It means that your inner world is ever-changing, as various elements **mingle with one another**, deepening your understanding and broadening your perspective.

  - With each new encounter, your mind evolves—absorbing, reflecting, and renewing itself.

- **"Mingle to Maintain":**

  As the process matures, you begin to settle into a state of balance.

  - **Maintaining** refers to stabilizing that dynamic energy, ensuring that the creative interplay of thoughts and experiences leads to a harmonious state.

  - This stage is about cultivating consistency and retaining the wisdom gained from the mingling of diverse influences.

- **"Maintain to Minus":**

  Here, you learn to discern what is essential from what is superfluous.

  - **Minus** represents the process of letting go—subtracting the unnecessary, the transient, and the clutter that hinders your growth.

  - It is the purification of your inner state, where you shed excess baggage and distractions.

- **"Minus to Maintain":**

  Finally, in this refined state, you re-establish balance.

  - After subtracting the inessential, what remains is a pure, stable essence that you can uphold.

  - **Maintaining** again in this context means that you preserve the clarity and simplicity that has emerged after the process of elimination.

In essence, child, this chain of words describes the journey of inner alchemy:

1. **Embrace and blend** all that life offers (Mix to Mingle).

2. **Allow these experiences to interact continuously** (Mingle to Mingle).

3. **Stabilize the lessons learned** (Mingle to Maintain).

4. **Discard the impurities and non-essentials** (Maintain to Minus).

5. **Sustain the pure, refined state of your being** (Minus to Maintain).

This cycle is not linear but a dynamic dance, where every stage feeds into the next, leading you ever closer to your true self.

May you always have the courage to mix, the wisdom to mingle, and the strength to maintain what is essential, so that the divine clarity within you shines forth.

Chapter-47

Paradox of Masters

The paradox of masters lies in their profound ability to be both deeply immersed in the world and yet detached from it. They walk among us, sharing their wisdom, offering guidance, and serving as beacons of light. To the world, they appear as teachers, leaders, and saviors, but in their essence, they are beyond all worldly roles and labels. A true master is not bound by time, space, or ego. They transcend the limitations of the physical world and reveal the divine within all things.

The paradox becomes clear when we realize that the master's true power lies in their ability to give without attachment, to lead without ego, and to teach without the need for recognition. They do not seek fame, wealth, or praise, for their fulfilment comes from the eternal peace that arises from surrender to the divine. In their presence, we see that wisdom is not about accumulating knowledge but about realizing the truth of who we are beyond the body and mind. A master embodies the highest truth: that all is one, that we are not separate from the divine but a reflection of it. Their life is a living example of divine harmony, showing us that by letting go of our attachments, we too can experience the same freedom, peace, and love. Through the paradox of their being, they guide us to the ultimate realization—that in surrendering the self, we become one with the eternal.

** ** **

Swamy, it isn't easy to understand when you suddenly said to yourself,

"They are masters, but they are not masters."

My question is: Who are you referring to with this statement? Why does it seem contradictory, and what is its inner message? Please explain so that I may understand.

Swamy's Spirit Speaks:

Child, this statement is a paradox meant to unveil the deeper truth of mastery. When I say, **"They are masters, but they are not masters,"** I point to the difference between **apparent mastery** and **true mastery**.

- **Apparent Mastery:**

  In the world, many individuals may hold titles, positions, or skills that seem to make them masters—experts in their fields, leaders in society, or teachers of certain arts. They have achieved a level of control or knowledge over a part of life. Yet, their mastery is limited to that aspect; it is **conditional** and often bound by ego, personal ambition, or social status.

- **True Mastery:**

  True mastery transcends any external label. It is the state of having conquered one's inner turmoil, ego, and attachments. A true master **serves without seeking to rule, teaches without clinging to authority, and remains humble despite his wisdom.**

  - They understand that **real power lies in surrendering the illusion of control.**

  - They are masters not in the sense of dominating the world, but in the sense of being completely free within it.

  - In this light, the apparent contradiction dissolves: those who appear to be masters in the conventional sense are, in the deeper truth, not masters at all, because true mastery is marked by the absence of the need to claim mastery.

The Inner Message:

- **Beyond Labels:**

  The statement urges you to look beyond conventional titles. A person's true worth is measured not by how much control or recognition they command, but by how deeply they have mastered themselves.

- **Humility and Service:**

  A genuine master remains humble. They do not flaunt their wisdom; instead, they serve as instruments of the divine without attachment to their role.

- **Transcending Duality:**

  In the realm of true spiritual insight, opposites merge. Mastery and the lack thereof are not opposing forces but are two expressions of the same truth: the journey from controlling to surrendering, from ego to unity.

Child, when you understand that **true mastery is a state of inner freedom and humility,** you will see that the apparent masters—those who claim control—are, in the highest sense, not masters at all. Their external achievements do not touch the inner essence, which remains unbound and pure.

May this insight guide you to seek the profound truth within yourself, where mastery is not about power, but about surrender and service.

Chapter-48
Silent Service

Silent service is the embodiment of pure selflessness, where the act of giving is not accompanied by any need for recognition or reward. It is the deep, silent rhythm of nature itself, where every element, from the earth to the sky, plays its part without expectation. The pancha bhoothas—earth, water, fire, air, and ether—work together in perfect harmony, silently sustaining life on this planet. The earth nourishes, the water cleanses, the fire transforms, the air breathes life, and the ether connects all. In this same way, silent service flows naturally from a heart that recognizes its connection to the divine presence within all things.

True fulfilment comes not from what we receive but from what we give. Just as the Pancha booths serve without ego or expectation, silent service invites us to act in the same way. The earth offers its resources without question, the water quenches our thirst without hesitation, and the wind carries the fragrance of life across the world—all without asking for anything in return. When we serve silently, without attachment to the outcome, we align ourselves with the natural forces that govern life. In doing so, we cultivate peace and harmony within ourselves and in the world around us. Silent service, like the pancha bhoothas, is a reflection of the divine, flowing effortlessly through us and into the world, transforming lives with its quiet power. Through this service, we realize that by giving, we too become part of the eternal cycle of life, contributing to the greater good and finding fulfilment in the simplest, most profound acts of kindness.

** ** **

Swamy, you always ask all your followers, **"Help the Poor, but don't advertise."** This seems to suggest that one should act selflessly without seeking recognition. What message are you truly communicating with these words?

Swamy's Spirit Speaks:

Child, when I say, **"Help the Poor, but don't advertise,"** I am inviting you to engage in pure, selfless service. Allow me to explain:

- **"Help the Poor":**

  This is a call to extend your compassion and assistance to those in need. It is not merely a social duty but a spiritual practice—an opportunity to dissolve the barriers of ego by recognizing the divine in every being.

  - When you help, you uplift not only those you serve but also your own spirit, as your actions become a reflection of inner love and generosity.

- **"But don't advertise":**

  This part of the instruction is equally important. True service must come without the desire for recognition, praise, or material gain.

  - Advertising your good deeds often shifts the focus from genuine compassion to personal pride. It transforms a sacred act into a performance for the world, thereby diluting its purity.

  - When your service remains unadvertised, it stays rooted in sincerity and humility—qualities that are essential for spiritual growth.

- **The Deeper Message:**

  In this world, many actions are driven by the need for external validation, which only feeds the ego. I urge you to transcend this tendency.

- **Serve without expecting anything in return.**

- **Let your actions be guided solely by love and the desire to alleviate suffering.**

- In doing so, you not only honor the poor but also honor your own inner divinity.

Child, the essence is simple yet profound: **act with a pure heart, let your service be its own reward, and allow the light of compassion to shine quietly from within.**

May you always serve selflessly and embrace the true spirit of humility.

Chapter-49

Living by His Design

Living by His design means aligning our lives with the divine blueprint that has been set for us, a path that reflects our true purpose and connection to the higher power. It's about recognizing that we are not isolated beings, but part of a greater, harmonious flow of existence. Every moment, every action, and every decision we make carries an opportunity to live in tune with this divine plan. It's easy to get caught up in the hustle and bustle of life, to pursue personal goals, and to chase after fleeting desires, but living by His design invites us to step back and listen—to the still voice within, to the guidance of the universe, and to the wisdom of the divine that is always present, even in the most ordinary moments.

When we live by His design, we free ourselves from the pressure of self-imposed expectations and the illusions of control. We surrender to the flow of life, trusting that each step we take is part of a grander purpose. This doesn't mean we abandon responsibility, but instead, we learn to work in harmony with the greater forces at play. It is about recognizing that our unique talents, experiences, and challenges are not random but are part of a divine plan meant to shape us into who we are destined to become. Living by His design brings peace, clarity, and fulfilment as we stop struggling against the current of life and instead trust in the divine wisdom guiding us every day. Through surrender and trust, we align ourselves with the higher will, finding joy and contentment in knowing that we are always on the right path.

** ** **

Swamy, during our interaction, you mentioned:

"We all came to earth, it is a beautiful thing, to enjoy all His things in the right way given by Him, to help His needful children in good and needful manner."

Although I have a general grasp of this message, I humbly request you to explain in detail what you mean by these words and how we can achieve such a state.

Swamy's Spirit Speaks:

Child, this message is an invitation to see our earthly journey as a divine opportunity—a gift from the Creator to experience, enjoy, and uplift life in its true essence. Allow me to break it down for you:

- **"We all came to earth"**

    - You must understand that our arrival on this earth is not by chance. It is a deliberate, sacred event.

    - Each soul is here to experience life, to learn, and to evolve. Our presence is a unique opportunity to explore the beauty and lessons of this world.

- **"It is a beautiful thing"**

    - Earth is a manifestation of divine creativity—a place where nature, relationships, and experiences offer infinite beauty.

    - Recognize the wonder in the simple things: the sunrise, the laughter of children, the compassion of a friend. These are reflections of the Divine.

- **"To enjoy all His things in the right way given by Him"**

    - Enjoyment here is not about indulgence or excess; it is about appreciating and using what is provided by the Divine with wisdom and balance.

    - **Right way** means living in harmony with the natural order—using resources responsibly, honouring nature, and cultivating gratitude in every moment.

- o It is the art of savouring life without falling into greed, selfishness, or waste.

- **"To help His needful children in good and needful manner"**

  - o This calls for service and compassion. The "needful children" represent all those in our world who are struggling, whether materially, emotionally, or spiritually.

  - o Helping others is not a mere act of charity; it is an expression of love and a duty to recognize the Divine in every being.

  - o **Good and needful manner** implies offering genuine, thoughtful support that respects the dignity of those you serve, rather than merely giving out of pity or obligation.

How to Achieve This:

1. **Cultivate Inner Awareness:**

   - o Begin with self-reflection. Understand your own gifts, limitations, and true needs.

   - o Develop mindfulness to recognize the beauty around you and within you.

2. **Practice Balanced Enjoyment:**

   - o Appreciate and use the resources at your disposal with moderation and gratitude.

   - o Avoid extremes—excessive indulgence dulls the senses, while deprivation can lead to hardship.

3. **Live in Harmony with Nature:**

   - o Respect the natural world as a sacred expression of the Divine.

   - o Adopt sustainable habits that honor the environment and the balance of life.

4. **Serve Others with Compassion:**

   - Look for opportunities to help those in need, not for recognition, but as an act of heartfelt service.

   - Be attentive to the unique needs of others, offering support that empowers rather than creates dependency.

5. **Embrace the Divine Perspective:**

   - Recognize that your journey on earth is part of a larger cosmic plan.

   - Trust that every experience—joy or challenge—is an opportunity for growth and deeper connection with the Divine.

Child, when you live with this balanced approach—enjoying life's gifts responsibly and extending compassionate service—you align yourself with the eternal truth. Your life becomes a celebration of beauty, a practice of mindful enjoyment, and a commitment to uplifting others.

May you walk this path with an open heart, recognizing that every moment on earth is a precious chance to experience the Divine in its fullness and to reflect that light in the lives of those around you.

Chapter-50

Essence of Truth

The essence of truth is simple yet profound—it is the unchanging reality that exists beyond our perceptions, beliefs, and judgments. Truth is not something that can be shaped or altered by our desires or fears; it remains constant, untouched by time or circumstance. It is the foundation of all that is real, the core of our existence, and the essence of everything that surrounds us. We often search for truth in external things, in what others say, or in what we see and hear, but true truth is found within ourselves, in the silence of our hearts, and in the clarity of our consciousness.

When we live in alignment with the essence of truth, we are not swayed by illusions or falsehoods. We see the world as it truly is, beyond the veils of judgment and preconceptions.

The truth does not demand anything from us; it simply is. It is through connecting with this inner truth that we find peace, clarity, and understanding. As we shed the layers of ego, fear, and attachment, we begin to experience the world with greater wisdom and compassion. In its purest form, truth is not just an intellectual understanding—it is a lived experience, a state of being, and a way of seeing the world. To embrace the essence of truth is to live authentically, to align our actions with what is right, and to remain grounded in the reality of what is eternal and unchanging.

** ** **

Swamy, you speak a few words that seem simple at first glance. One such phrase is,

"Fact is a Fact."

I understand its literal meaning, yet I sense there is a deeper intention behind it when you declare these words. Is there something you want to communicate to society through this statement?

Swamy's Spirit Speaks:

Child, the phrase **"Fact is a Fact"** may appear straightforward, but it carries a profound call to recognize and honor the immutable truth in life. Let me reveal its deeper essence:

- **Immutable Truth:**

  - A fact, by definition, is an unchanging reality.

  - This statement reminds you that certain truths exist independent of our opinions, desires, or interpretations.

  - In a world of shifting perspectives, acknowledging that **"Fact is a Fact"** is a call to ground yourself in reality as it is.

- **A Call for Honesty:**

  - When you affirm that a fact remains a fact, you reject the distortion of truth for personal gain or convenience.

  - It is an invitation for society to value transparency and integrity, even when the truth is inconvenient or harsh.

- **A Message to Overcome Delusion:**

  - In many situations, people may prefer to cling to comforting illusions rather than face reality.

  - By stating **"Fact is a Fact,"** I urge you to confront reality with courage and clarity, understanding that growth and transformation begin with accepting the truth.

- **Foundation for Social Change:**

  - On a societal level, this phrase is a reminder that progress is built on acknowledging reality, not on denying it.

  - True reform and evolution can only take root when everyone accepts the unvarnished facts of a situation, no matter how challenging they may be.

Child, the essence of **"Fact is a Fact"** is to encourage you—and society—to let truth be the guiding light. Stand firm in the face of illusion, embrace the reality that surrounds you, and let this truth pave the way for ethical choices and meaningful change.

May you always have the courage to face the truth, and may the light of unaltered facts guide you in every step of your journey.

Chapter-51
Rama: The Truth Incarnate

Rama, the divine prince of Ayodhya, is revered as the embodiment of truth, righteousness, and dharma. He is not just a historical figure or mythological hero but a living manifestation of truth itself. His life and actions offer timeless lessons on the values of integrity, duty, and virtue. Rama's commitment to truth is unwavering, even when faced with immense trials and personal sacrifices. In his journey, he shows that following the path of truth is not always the easiest, but it is always the noblest. Rama's choices were guided by dharma—righteous action—and he demonstrated through his actions that truth is not a mere concept but a force that shapes reality.

Rama's devotion to dharma is seen in his ability to make decisions based on the highest ethical standards, regardless of personal pain or hardship. His exile to the forest, the sacrifice of his kingdom, and his unwavering adherence to his principles even in the face of betrayal all speak to the profound depth of his commitment to truth. For Rama, truth was not a relative notion—it was the foundation of his existence, something to be upheld at any cost. Through his character, he reveals that living in alignment with the truth of one's purpose leads to true peace and fulfilment.

In spiritual terms, Rama is often referred to as "Maryada Purushottama," the supreme being who sets the boundaries of righteousness and moral conduct. His life exemplifies the essence of dharma—maintaining balance and harmony in the world while remaining true to one's higher calling. By embodying truth in every aspect of his life, Rama teaches us that we too can overcome adversity and live a life of virtue. Just as the sun's light illuminates the world, the truth embodied by Rama lights the way for all those who seek guidance. His legacy continues to inspire millions, reminding us that living by the truth—no matter the circumstance—brings us closer to the divine and reveals the eternal wisdom of the universe.

**** ** ****

Swamy, you once said,

"Truth is Rama, Truth is God."

Why do you mention only Rama in this context, and not Krishna, Jesus, or Bala Tripura? Is there a specific intention or context behind choosing Rama to represent Truth? Please explain so that we may understand the deeper meaning behind these words.

Swamy's Spirit Speaks:

Child, when I declare **"Truth is Rama, Truth is God,"** I am using the name "Rama" as a symbol—a luminous emblem of righteousness, integrity, and the unwavering commitment to truth. In our spiritual heritage, Rama is revered not merely as a historical figure, but as the embodiment of divine truth and dharma. His life, marked by virtue, honor, and compassion, serves as a timeless guide for living in accordance with the highest ideals.

Let me explain further:

- **Rama as the Embodiment of Truth:**
  - Rama exemplifies an ideal of truth that is clear, steadfast, and free from ego.
  - He stands as a model for all who seek to live righteously—his name conveys not only personal virtue but the universal quality of truth itself.

- By saying **"Truth is Rama,"** I encourage you to see that the truth you seek is not abstract or distant; it is embodied in the virtues that Rama represents.

- **Why Not Other Names?**

  - You may wonder why I do not invoke Krishna, Jesus, or Bala Tripura. Each of these revered names indeed represents aspects of the Divine:

    - **Krishna** shines with playful wisdom and divine love.

    - **Jesus** embodies sacrificial love and redemption.

    - **Bala Tripura** reveals the creative and nurturing facets of the Divine.

  - However, in this context, I choose **Rama** because his example focuses on the resolute adherence to truth and the unwavering pursuit of dharma.

  - Rama's life teaches us that truth is not a matter of opinion or interpretation—it is an unchangeable, guiding light. When you align with truth, you are aligning with the Divine, irrespective of the form in which it appears.

- **The Universal Essence:**

  - Understand that whether you call upon Rama, Krishna, Jesus, or any other name, the essence remains the same: **Truth is God.**

  - Each name points to the same ultimate reality, expressed through different qualities and teachings.

  - My mention of Rama is intended to highlight a particular aspect of that truth—namely, its clarity, its commitment to righteousness, and its role as a beacon for ethical living.

Child, let these words inspire you to seek the truth within yourself, to see that truth as a divine light that guides every action, every thought, and every moment of your life. In doing so, you will realize that all paths, though varied in form, lead to the same eternal reality.

May you always remain steadfast in the pursuit of truth, and may the divine light of righteousness shine upon your path.

Chapter-52

Inner vs. Outer

The concept of "Inner vs. Outer" speaks to the dichotomy between our inner world—our thoughts, emotions, and spirit—and the outer world—our external circumstances, relationships, and material possessions. In today's fast-paced society, much of our focus tends to be on the outer world. We become preoccupied with our achievements, appearances, and material success, often overlooking the deeper, more meaningful aspects of our existence. The outer world is often in flux, influenced by external forces beyond our control. It can be tempting to base our sense of happiness and fulfilment on outer achievements and validations, but this approach is often fleeting and unstable.

The inner world, on the other hand, is where true peace, wisdom, and strength reside. Our thoughts, beliefs, and emotional state shape how we experience the world around us. When we look inward, we connect with our higher self, our purpose, and our deeper understanding of life. The inner world is constant and unchanging, providing a solid foundation for navigating the ever-changing outer world. True contentment does not come from external possessions or recognition, but from cultivating peace, balance, and clarity within ourselves.

Spiritual teachings often emphasize the importance of nurturing the inner world, as it is through self-awareness, self-reflection, and inner growth that we are able to transcend the superficial aspects of life. When we align our inner world with our outer actions, we create harmony between the two. The true path to happiness lies not in the accumulation of external wealth or status, but in the cultivation of inner peace, wisdom, and compassion. By turning inward, we find that the external world loses its power to control us. We begin to see beyond the distractions, focusing instead on living in alignment with our authentic self and with the greater truth that binds us all. In this way, the inner and outer worlds are not separate, but interconnected—and by mastering the inner, we shape a more fulfilling outer life.

** ** **

Swamy, you once stated,

"Compare inside and outside power and status, don't compare. Don't copy. Compose yourself."

These words are both instructive and thought-provoking. While they sound educative, I feel there is a deeper, unique message behind them. Could you please explain what you mean by this, so that we may understand the inner essence and apply it in our lives?

Swamy's Spirit Speaks:

Child, these words are meant to guide you away from the pitfalls of external validation and toward the nurturing of your inner self. Let me break down the message for you:

- **"Compare inside and outside power and status":**

  - **Outside Power and Status:**

    In the world, society often measures worth by external factors—wealth, influence, titles, and appearances. These are fleeting and can create feelings of inadequacy or superiority when you compare yourself with others.

  - **Inside Power and Status:**

    Your true strength and worth come from within. This inner power is built on virtues such as wisdom, compassion, integrity, and self-awareness. It is the enduring, unchanging essence of who you are.

- **"Don't compare. Don't copy."**

  - **Avoid Comparison:**

    When you compare yourself with others, you invite dissatisfaction and envy. Each person's journey is unique, and no external measure can capture the richness of your inner experience.

  - **Avoid Imitation:**

    To copy another's way of life is to deny your own individuality. Authentic growth comes from embracing your unique qualities rather than mimicking someone else's path.

- **"Compose Yourself."**

  - This is an invitation to create and nurture your own inner harmony.

  - **Compose Yourself** means to gather your thoughts, align your actions with your inner truth, and build a life that reflects your unique potential.

  - It is about finding balance and integrity within, so that your external actions naturally flow from a well-cultivated inner world.

The Inner Essence:

Child, the essence of my words is a call to prioritize your inner development over superficial measures of success.

- Recognize that true power lies in the inner self—the qualities that remain constant despite the ever-changing external world.

- Do not allow the world's transient standards to dictate your worth. Instead, nurture and develop your unique strengths and virtues.

- When you compose yourself, you become the author of your own life, guided by inner truth rather than by the shifting opinions of others.

May you always strive to build your inner world with care and let your authentic self shine, unburdened by comparison or imitation.

Chapter-53

The Sacred Path of Directions

In spiritual teachings, directions often symbolize more than just physical pathways or geographical bearings; they represent the flow of energy, wisdom, and divine guidance in our lives. The sacred path of directions is a metaphor for the spiritual journey that we all embark upon. Each direction— North, South, East, and West—holds its own significance and invites us to explore different aspects of our existence and consciousness. These directions are not just physical orientations but are symbolic of the spiritual and internal realms we navigate in our pursuit of truth.

The East, often associated with the rising sun, symbolizes the dawn of enlightenment and new beginnings. It is the direction of birth and renewal, the place where divine wisdom enters our lives. In this space, we are invited to cultivate spiritual awareness, seeking the truth that illuminates our path. The South, associated with warmth and nurturing, teaches us the importance of growth, compassion, and love. This direction encourages us to connect with our hearts, nurturing relationships and fostering empathy and kindness in our actions. The West, where the sun sets, reminds us of the cycles of life and death, and the importance of transformation and release. It calls us to embrace impermanence and to let go of attachments that hinder our growth, preparing us for the spiritual rebirth that awaits. Finally, the North is often seen as the direction of wisdom, strength, and stability. It represents the inner strength we cultivate through discipline and dedication, providing us with the foundation to continue our journey with resilience and grace.

In a spiritual sense, the sacred path of directions teaches us how to balance the various aspects of life—our mind, heart, body, and soul. It calls us to align our actions with the principles of dharma, to move forward with integrity, and to honor the sacredness in all things. The journey is not a linear one; rather, it is cyclical, where each direction offers its lessons, guiding us toward wholeness. By understanding and embracing these directions, we are reminded that life is a sacred path—one that requires our attention, our mindfulness, and our connection to the divine presence that resides within us and around us. Ultimately, the sacred path of directions leads us to discover our true purpose and divine essence, helping us find peace and fulfilment in every step we take.

**** ** ****

Swamy, you often speak of directions by saying,

"North and East are Positive Directions, South is Negative, and West is Neutral."

My question is: if God resides in all directions, why should there be such deviations or distractions? Please explain.

Swamy's Spirit Speaks:

Child, the statement about directions is not a literal division of the Divine but a symbolic guide to the different energetic qualities that influence our lives. Let me explain:

- **Symbolic Significance of the Directions:**
  - **North and East as Positive:**
    - The East, where the sun rises, symbolizes new beginnings, illumination, and inspiration.
    - The North represents stability, wisdom, and a steady progression toward higher truth.
    - Together, these directions remind you to seek and align with energies that uplift and inspire you.

- ○ **South as Negative:**

  - The South, symbolically, points to challenges and obstacles.

  - It represents the forces that pull you downward, the trials that test your strength and resolve.

  - However, these challenges are opportunities for growth—they are the pressures that refine your inner self, much like fire purifies gold.

- ○ **West as Neutral:**

  - The West signifies balance—a space where both light and shadow coexist.

  - It encourages you to reflect on your experiences without bias, helping you to integrate the lessons of both success and struggle.

- **The Universal Presence of God:**

  - ○ Although these directions symbolize different energies, remember that **God is omnipresent and transcends all these boundaries.**

  - ○ The Divine resides in every direction and every aspect of creation; these symbols are simply tools to help you understand and balance the various influences in your life.

- **Navigating Life's Energies:**

  - ○ Use the positive energies of the North and East as your guiding lights to inspire and motivate you.

  - ○ Recognize the lessons in the challenges of the South as opportunities to grow stronger and wiser.

  - ○ Embrace the neutrality of the West to cultivate balance and clarity in your perceptions.

  - ○ These distinctions are not meant to limit your understanding of the Divine but to offer you a framework for living in harmony with the dynamic flow of life.

Child, while it may seem that these directional qualities impose limitations, they are only symbolic markers that help you discern the energies around you. In truth, **the Divine is one, unbounded by any direction, yet it expresses itself in myriad ways through these natural symbols.**

May you always see beyond the symbols to the infinite light that pervades all, and may you find balance and wisdom in every direction of your journey.

SILENCE AS THE GATEWAY

(Tapping into Profound Stillness to Access Higher
States of Consciousness)

Chapter-54

The Ocean of Stillness

In a world where success is often quantified by numbers, achievements, and measurable outcomes, there exists a deeper dimension of life that transcends all forms of measurement. True fulfilment, peace, and love cannot be confined to scales or comparisons; they are boundless, infinite, and immeasurable. To live beyond measure is to embrace the vastness of life in its purest form, where joy, compassion, and wisdom are experienced without the need for validation or applause. It is in this space where we learn to be content with what is, rather than always striving for more.

When we move beyond measure, we release the constraints of societal expectations and personal limitations. We recognize that the essence of life cannot be boxed into accomplishments, wealth, or recognition. Instead, it flourishes in our connection to the present moment, to our own heart, and to the world around us. Living beyond measure is about cultivating an inner peace that remains unaffected by external circumstances. It is about finding value in the intangible—the love we give, the kindness we extend, and the wisdom we share. In doing so, we experience a life that is richer than any measure can quantify, one that is guided by authenticity, grace, and the pursuit of spiritual growth.

** ** **

Swamy, you simply pass a statement that appears simple at first glance, but when we try to capture its essence, we become lost. What do you mean by,

"Media and Charity is not countable"?

I understand the individual words, yet I sense there is a deeper message here. Is there something specific you wish to communicate to society through this statement? Please explain its inner essence.

Swamy's Spirit Speaks:

Child, when I say **"Media and Charity is not countable,"** I invite you to look beyond the surface and understand that the true value of both lies not in numerical measures or material accumulation, but in their qualitative, transformative power. Allow me to explain:

- **Media Beyond Numbers:**

  - **Media** represents all the channels—be it words, art, or technology—through which truth and wisdom are shared.

  - Its impact is not found in ratings, views, or monetary gains, but in the **depth of transformation** it brings to the heart and mind.

  - When you use media to communicate divine truths, you engage in a process that transcends quantification; its true worth is felt rather than counted.

- **Charity Beyond Counting:**

  - **Charity** is the act of giving from a place of pure love and selflessness.

  - The real essence of charity is not measured by how much you give, but by the **purity of your intention** and the **spirit in which you serve.**

  - True charity does not keep score—it flows naturally from a heart filled with compassion. Its value is seen in the transformation it inspires, not in the numbers on a ledger.

- **The Deeper Message:**

  - Both media and charity, when imbued with divine intent, become vehicles for spiritual awakening.

- ○ They are tools that help dissolve the boundaries between the self and the other, enabling a flow of wisdom and love that cannot be confined to figures or statistics.

- ○ In this context, "not countable" means that the impact of genuine media and heartfelt charity is immeasurable—it is the quality of life they uplift, the inner light they kindle, and the unity they foster among people.

Child, I urge you to look beyond conventional measures. Understand that the true worth of our expressions and our giving is in the **spiritual transformation** they inspire. When you share with a pure heart, when you communicate with wisdom, you touch lives in ways that numbers can never capture.

May you always strive to express and give in ways that enrich the soul, knowing that the true impact of your actions is infinite and beyond counting.

Chapter-55

Silent Devotion

Silent devotion is the purest form of worship, a language that transcends words and speaks directly to the soul. It is in the quiet moments of reflection and prayer that we connect deeply with the divine. No grand gestures, no loud proclamations— just a stillness that speaks louder than any spoken prayer could. In silence, we listen, not only to the whispers of our heart but to the echoes of the universe itself.

This devotion is not about external show, but about an internal surrender. When we devote ourselves silently, we are not seeking recognition or reward. We are simply offering our hearts, in their purest form, to the divine. It is in these moments of silence that we truly understand the meaning of faith— when words are no longer necessary, and the divine presence is felt in every breath, in every heartbeat.

Spirituality is often not about how much we say, but about how much we feel. Silent devotion speaks the language of love, purity, and surrender. It is through silence that we experience the deepest connection to our higher selves and to the divine source of all. In the stillness, we find our truest form of devotion—one that is unspoken, yet infinitely profound.

** ** **

Swamy, you once said,

"God is silence, God is everything. Dedicate to Him, dedicate to Him, dive in Him, derive Him, drive Him in all body."

These words are wonderful and inspiring. I ask: How can one truly achieve this state? It seems that such a transformation occurs not by our own will alone, but when His will coincides with ours and His grace manifests in us. Please explain the inner process behind these words and how we can align our will with the Divine Will to realize this vision.

Swamy's Spirit Speaks:

Child, these words point to the profound process of integrating the Divine into every fiber of your being. Let me share the essence of each phrase:

- **"God is silence, God is everything":**
  - This reveals that the Divine is both the quiet, unmanifest presence and the vibrant, all-pervading reality of life.
  - In silence, you find the space where the Divine dwells, and in everything, you see the reflection of that ultimate truth.

- **"Dedicate to Him, dedicate to Him":**
  - Dedication means offering your whole self to the Divine—not half-heartedly, but with unwavering commitment.
  - This repeated call reinforces that true transformation begins when you surrender your ego and make the Divine the center of your life.

- **"Dive in Him":**
  - To dive in Him is to immerse yourself completely in divine meditation and devotion.
  - It is an invitation to let go of superficial desires and to plunge deep into the ocean of spiritual truth, where the boundaries of self dissolve.

- **"Derive Him":**
  - This means extracting the essence of the Divine in every experience.

- ○ Look at life as a continuous opportunity to learn from the Divine—the lessons in nature, in relationships, in every breath.

- ○ When you derive the Divine, you transform everyday moments into sacred insights.

- **"Drive Him in all body":**

  - ○ To drive the Divine in all body is to let His energy permeate your entire being.

  - ○ This is achieved through disciplined practices, such as meditation, prayer, and selfless service, which align your physical, mental, and spiritual energies with the Divine Will.

Now, you ask how one can achieve this state. Understand that:

- **It is not by sheer human effort alone:**

  - ○ When you try to impose your will, the limited ego may resist, and the process stalls.

  - ○ True transformation unfolds when you surrender and allow the grace of the Divine to work within you.

- **Alignment of Will:**

  - ○ The magic happens when your inner desire, your sincere longing for truth, aligns with the Divine Will.

  - ○ In that harmonious state, obstacles vanish and the natural flow of grace transforms you from within.

- **Practical Steps for Alignment:**

  - ○ **Surrender:** Let go of rigid attachments and open your heart completely to the Divine.

  - ○ **Meditate Deeply:** Create moments of silence in which you can listen to the subtle whisper of divine guidance.

  - ○ **Live with Devotion:** Allow every action, word, and thought to reflect your commitment to a higher purpose.

- **Practice Self-Discipline:** Cultivate habits that purify your body, mind, and spirit, making them a receptive vessel for divine energy.

Child, remember that this journey is gradual. The Divine does not force transformation; it unfolds naturally when you are ready to merge your will with His. In that merging, you become an instrument of His grace, and the fullness of His presence is manifest in your life.

May you always trust in the process, surrender to His grace, and walk your path with a heart open to the infinite light of the Divine.

DISSOLVING THE SELF

(Moving beyond personal identity to experience
the formless essence of being)

Chapter-56

Priceless Gifts

*The most precious gifts in life come without a price tag—
bestowed upon us by nature, given freely, without expectation.
The sun rises each day, offering warmth and light, never asking
for gratitude. The trees stand silently, giving shade, fruit,
and shelter, never keeping count of their offerings. The rivers
flow, quenching thirst and nourishing life, without choosing
whom to serve. Such is the way of true giving—effortless,
unconditional, and selfless.*

*Wisdom teaches us that the highest form of giving mirrors
nature's way—giving without attachment, loving without
conditions, serving without seeking recognition. Like the
squirrel that buries seeds, unaware that it is planting forests
for the future, our smallest acts of kindness ripple through
existence in ways we may never see.*

*In a world obsessed with wealth and possessions, let
us cherish these priceless gifts—the gentle breeze, the
endless sky, the silent embrace of the earth. And above
all, let us learn from them—to give, to serve, and to love,
without expecting anything in return. For in such selfless
acts, we discover the deepest joy—the joy of being in
harmony with life itself.*

** ** **

Swamy, you often refer to two precious words—**Sacrifice and
Self-Contentment**—as gifts from Lord Shiva. How do we truly
understand their essence?

Swamy's Spirit Speaks:

Child, these words are not mere concepts but profound spiritual tools that shape your inner journey. They are the very gifts that Lord Shiva, the embodiment of renunciation and transformation, bestows upon those who seek to awaken their true self. Let me explain their deeper meaning:

Sacrifice:

- **The Art of Letting Go:**

    - Sacrifice is the conscious act of relinquishing attachments, desires, and ego-driven pursuits.

    - It is not about loss or self-denial for its own sake but about making space for higher truths.

    - Just as a tree sheds its leaves in autumn to prepare for new growth, you must let go of what no longer serves your inner evolution.

- **A Path to Purity:**

    - When you sacrifice, you purify your heart and mind, removing the clutter of selfishness and material cravings.

    - This purification allows the divine energy within you to shine more brightly, guiding you toward a state of inner freedom.

- **Living Selflessly:**

    - True sacrifice comes from a place of love—acting without expectation of reward.

    - It is the essence of service, where every action is offered as a gift to the Divine, much like the selfless dance of Lord Shiva, who transforms the world through his cosmic rhythm.

Self-Contentment:

- **Inner Satisfaction:**

  - Self-contentment is the state of being truly satisfied with what you have, independent of external circumstances.

  - It is an inner calm that arises when you recognize that true happiness does not come from external achievements but from the peace and fulfilment within your own heart.

- **Freedom from Desire:**

  - When you cultivate self-contentment, you free yourself from the endless cycle of craving and discontent.

  - This state of contentment allows you to appreciate the present moment and see the beauty in every experience, without constantly chasing after more.

- **A Reflection of Inner Wisdom:**

  - Self-contentment is not complacency—it is the mature understanding that the journey itself is enough.

  - It is a gift that enables you to live in harmony with your true nature, accepting life as it unfolds with grace and humility.

Interconnection and the Path Forward:

- **The Dance of Sacrifice and Self-Contentment:**

  - These two virtues are deeply intertwined. When you practice sacrifice, you shed the burdens of ego and desire, which paves the way for true self-contentment.

  - In turn, self-contentment strengthens your resolve to sacrifice further as you come to realize that lasting joy is found not in accumulation but in the simplicity of being.

- **Embodying the Gifts of Lord Shiva:**

  - Embrace sacrifice as a way to clear away the unnecessary and focus on what truly matters.

- Cultivate self-contentment by finding gratitude in the present moment and recognizing the divine in every aspect of life.

- As you internalize these gifts, you move closer to the state of liberation that Lord Shiva represents—a state where the mind is free, the heart is open, and life is lived in balance with the cosmic flow.

Child, remember that these are not merely abstract ideals but practical steps on your path to spiritual awakening. Let sacrifice be the gentle clearing of the old, and let self-contentment be the serene acceptance of the now. In this union, you will discover that your true wealth is the light within you, guiding every step on your journey.

May you always find the strength to let go, the wisdom to be content, and the grace to walk the path of the Divine, embodying the eternal gifts of sacrifice and self-contentment.

Chapter-57

Honour the Silent Sacrifice

A mother's love is deep and silent, like the roots of a tree that hold everything together but remain unseen. She gives without asking, endures without complaining, and carries the weight of her family with quiet strength. Just like the earth nourishes life without seeking gratitude, a mother nurtures her children without expecting anything in return. The river flows tirelessly, quenching thirst without making a sound, and the sun rises each day, giving warmth without asking for recognition. In the same way, a mother's sacrifices often go unnoticed, yet they shape our lives in the most profound ways. Her love is not in grand gestures but in the everyday moments of care, patience, and selflessness.

**** ** ****

Swamy, during your discourse, you addressed the youth with a profound statement: **"A father is a great man who sacrifices his life, hides his feelings, ignores his happiness, accepts pain, forgets his comfort, and struggles tirelessly so that his children may live comfortably and happily without struggle. So, do not hurt your father—pat him gently."** What deeper message were you trying to convey?

Swamy's Spirit Speaks:

A father is not just a provider of food and shelter; he is the silent force that builds the foundation of a child's life. **His love is often unseen, his sacrifices unspoken, yet his presence is the pillar that holds everything together.** He walks through storms so his children may walk in the sunshine. He carries burdens so that their shoulders remain light.

Yet, in this journey, many fail to recognize the quiet sacrifices of a father. **His struggles are overlooked, his pain is dismissed, and his silent endurance is mistaken for indifference.** Children, lost in their own pursuits, often fail to see the weariness in his eyes, the calluses on his hands, or the unspoken dreams he gave up for their sake.

I said those words to awaken awareness, to stir gratitude in hearts that have taken a father's love for granted. Just as we gently handle something fragile, we must handle the emotions of a father with care. A simple word of love, a moment of appreciation, or a gentle pat on his back can become the warmth that eases his lifelong struggles.

Love is not just in receiving—it is in recognizing, appreciating, and giving back. When you honour the sacrifices of a father, you honour the very hands that shaped your destiny.

Chapter-58

Sharing is Caring

Sharing is one of the most powerful expressions of love, compassion, and connection. When we share, we open our hearts and allow others to experience the same joy, comfort, and support that we often seek for ourselves. It extends beyond material things—sharing includes our time, our knowledge, our kindness, and our presence. In a world that often emphasizes individuality and accumulation, sharing reminds us of our interconnectedness as human beings. It beautifully acknowledges that we are all part of a greater whole, and by giving, we contribute to the well-being of others and the world around us.

When we share, we are not losing anything; we are gaining much more—fulfilment, growth, and a sense of purpose. The act of giving expands our hearts and nourishes our spirits, drawing us closer to the essence of compassion and humanity. It strengthens our bonds with others, fostering unity, trust, and harmony. Sharing teaches us to look beyond our own desires and recognize the needs of those around us. In doing so, we create a ripple effect of positivity and kindness that spreads throughout the world. The more we share, the more we realize that true wealth lies not in what we keep, but in what we give. When we care enough to share, we help create a brighter, more compassionate world where everyone is uplifted.

Spiritual sharing transcends the material world and connects us on a deeper, soulful level. It's the sharing of wisdom, peace, and love that comes from within. When we share spiritually, we are not just offering advice or teachings; we are offering a reflection of our own divine essence, helping others awaken to their true nature. This kind of sharing creates an invisible bond that unites souls, transcending time, place, and circumstance. It is an act of surrendering our ego and allowing the light of truth to flow freely, without attachment. Just as a candle lights another without losing its flame, spiritual sharing ignites hearts, guiding others on their path to peace, joy, and enlightenment. Through sharing our spiritual experiences and insights, we contribute to the collective consciousness, elevating humanity and manifesting divine love in the world.

** ** **

Swamy, you addressed a group of your followers and said,

"Sharing is very very important."

I understand the surface meaning, but I sense there is a deeper essence behind these words. Could you please reveal the hidden essence so that we may understand, internalize, and practice it in our day-to-day lives?

Swamy's Spirit Speaks:

Child, the act of sharing is far more than the simple exchange of material things—it is a profound expression of our inner nature and connection to the Divine. Allow me to unveil its deeper meaning:

- **The Essence of Sharing:**

  Sharing is the natural outflow of a compassionate heart. When you share, you are not merely giving away what you have; you are expressing gratitude for the abundance in your life.

  - It is an acknowledgment that what you possess is not solely yours but a gift from the Divine meant to be circulated among all beings.

  - True sharing dissolves the barriers of selfishness and creates a flow of generosity that enriches both the giver and the receiver.

- **Internalizing the Practice:**

  To internalize sharing means to make it a part of your very being:

  - **Cultivate Selflessness:** Recognize that when you share, you are nurturing a spirit of unity and oneness. Let go of the ego that clings to possessions, and open your heart to the joy of giving.

  - **Extend Beyond Material Wealth:** Sharing is not limited to money or physical goods; it includes your time, knowledge, love, and kindness. A kind word, a listening ear, or a helping hand can be just as transformative.

  - **Live Generously:** Make sharing an everyday practice. In your interactions—at home, work, or within your community—allow your actions to reflect the abundance of your inner life.

- **The Transformative Power:**

  When you share, you create a ripple effect that transcends the immediate act:

  - **Healing and Connection:** Sharing helps mend divisions and build trust. It fosters a sense of community and belonging, reminding everyone that we are all interdependent.

  - **Spiritual Growth:** The more you give selflessly, the more you attune yourself to the divine flow. This not only benefits those around you but also enriches your own soul, paving the way for deeper inner transformation.

  - **Universal Abundance:** The act of sharing transforms scarcity into abundance. When you let go of what you hold tightly, you make room for more blessings to enter your life.

Child, remember that sharing is the language of love and the expression of our highest values. It is very, very important because it is through sharing that we break down the walls of isolation and discover our true interconnectedness.

May you practice sharing with a full heart, and in doing so, experience the joy and peace that comes from living in harmony with the Divine flow.

Chapter-59

Media Paradox

In today's world, media plays an undeniable role in shaping our perceptions, influencing our thoughts, and guiding our actions. It connects us to the world, informs us of what's happening around us, and has the power to mould public opinion. Yet, there lies a paradox: while it provides vast amounts of information, it often leaves us disconnected from the deeper truths of life. The very medium that promises to inform and enlighten can sometimes mislead or distract us from the essence of what truly matters. In this paradox, the more we are bombarded with external information, the more we can lose touch with our inner voice and wisdom.

Media thrives on sensationalism, trends, and narratives that often cater to superficial desires and immediate gratifications. It can distract us from the richness of human experience, pushing us to focus on external factors while ignoring the depths of our own consciousness. From a spiritual standpoint, this constant flood of external stimuli can lead to a state of confusion, making it difficult to hear the still, small voice of intuition and inner truth. The pursuit of worldly knowledge through media often overshadows the pursuit of self-awareness and spiritual awakening, causing us to become more attached to transient things than to the eternal nature of our soul.

Yet, media also has the potential to be a powerful tool for positive change. It can spread messages of peace, inspire social movements, and help us reflect on the greater purpose of life. The challenge, then, is to navigate the complexities of the media landscape with discernment and mindfulness. Spiritually, this requires a shift in perspective—recognizing

*that external noise can only reach us if we allow it to, and that
true wisdom comes from turning inward. By understanding
the paradox, we can use media not as a means of escaping
our reality, but as a channel for growth, awareness, and
connection to higher truths. When we align ourselves
spiritually, we can discern what truly contributes to our
soul's evolution and what merely feeds the ego. In this
way, media becomes a tool for enlightenment, guiding us
toward greater awareness, compassion, and inner peace
in a world filled with distractions.*

** ** **

Swamy, I know that you are different but never indifferent. I have sensed the meaning between your words. On one occasion, you told me,

"I need media, but I don't want media."

Swamy, please clarify what you meant by this statement so that common spiritual aspirants may understand its true essence.

Swamy's Spirit Speaks:

Child, this paradoxical phrase is meant to guide you in understanding the delicate balance between communication and distraction in the spiritual journey.

- **"I need media":**

  - The divine message must be shared; a channel is essential for it to reach the hearts of people.

  - Just as fire requires oxygen to burn, the truth needs a medium—be it art, literature, technology, or personal discourse—to illuminate souls and foster awakening.

- **"But I don't want media":**

  - While a channel is necessary, the external medium often carries superficiality, vanity, and distraction.

- Media in its worldly form can dilute or distort the pure message, turning spiritual wisdom into mere noise.

- I do not desire a media that overshadows the essence of truth with ego, sensationalism, or trivialities.

- **The Delicate Balance:**

  - The paradox lies in the fact that, although a vehicle is required to communicate divine truth, that vehicle must remain a humble servant rather than becoming an idol or an end in itself.

  - **True media** is a tool that helps disseminate wisdom without corrupting it; it must serve the message, not overshadow or redefine it.

Child, the message here is clear: **Embrace the means to communicate truth, but never allow the medium to become a distraction from the divine essence.**

Focus on the substance of your spiritual practice, ensuring that any form of expression or communication remains pure and serves only to illuminate the inner light.

May you always discern between the tool and the truth, using media wisely as a humble conduit for divine expression.

Chapter-60

Simple Living, Divine Trust

In a world that often values complexity, simple living is a return to the essentials—finding joy and fulfilment in what truly matters. It's about embracing the present moment, appreciating the beauty in simplicity, and recognizing that true wealth doesn't lie in material possessions but in inner peace, purpose, and connection. Living simply allows us to focus on what's meaningful and let go of unnecessary distractions.

Divine trust is the foundation upon which simple living thrives. It is the faith that the universe, or a higher power, has a plan for us, guiding our steps and providing what we need. When we trust in the divine, we release the need to control every outcome, and instead, surrender to the flow of life with openness and faith. This trust is not passive—it's an active belief that everything is unfolding as it should, even when the path isn't clear.

Together, simple living and divine trust create a life of grace. They invite us to let go of the burdens of overcomplication, embrace the blessings we have, and trust that the universe is supporting us in our journey. When we live with simplicity and trust, we find peace, clarity, and joy in every moment, knowing that we are held by something greater than ourselves

** ** **

Swamy, you often offer simple and inspiring solutions to complex problems. I recall you once said,

"Live simply, love generously, care deeply, speak kindly, and leave the rest to God."

Could you please explain the deeper essence of this statement with your grace, so that I may understand how to apply this wisdom in my life?

Swamy's Spirit Speaks:

Child, this statement is a timeless guide for finding inner peace and living a meaningful life. Each phrase carries a profound message that, when integrated, can transform the way you navigate the world. Let me break it down for you:

- **Live Simply:**
  - Simplicity is not about depriving yourself, but about focusing on what truly matters.
  - When you live simply, you remove unnecessary clutter—both materially and mentally—so that your energy can be directed toward what enriches your soul.
  - Think of it as clearing a garden of weeds to allow the flowers to flourish.

- **Love Generously:**
  - To love generously means to give love freely without expecting anything in return.
  - It is the practice of opening your heart wide to others, sharing kindness and compassion, even in the face of challenges.
  - This generous love not only nourishes those around you but also fills your own heart with joy and warmth.

- **Care Deeply:**
  - Caring deeply is about being genuinely concerned for the well-being of others.
  - It calls you to be empathetic and present, to listen, and to support without judgment.

- When you care deeply, you build connections that uplift both you and the people you encounter.

- **Speak Kindly:**

  - Your words have the power to heal or hurt. Speaking kindly means choosing language that is gentle, encouraging, and truthful.

  - This practice cultivates a positive environment and reflects the inner beauty of your character.

  - Just as a soft breeze can calm a storm, kind words can soothe troubled hearts.

- **Leave the Rest to God:**

  - This final phrase is an invitation to trust in the Divine plan.

  - After you have done your part by living simply, loving generously, caring deeply, and speaking kindly, release your worries and attachments about what lies beyond your control.

  - Trust that the universe, in its infinite wisdom, will take care of the rest, guiding you gently on your path.

Child, the secret of peace lies in this balanced approach. When you simplify your life, you create space for genuine love and care. When you express yourself with kindness and trust in the Divine, you find that life unfolds with grace and purpose. This holistic practice not only calms your inner world but also radiates positivity to those around you.

May you always nurture simplicity, generous love, deep care, and kind speech, and may you rest in the comforting assurance that the rest is lovingly taken care of by the Divine.

Chapter-61

Glow & Grow

To glow is to shine with authenticity and inner brilliance. It's about embracing your unique light and letting it shine brightly, unshaken by external circumstances. When we glow, we radiate positivity, confidence, and joy, not because of what we possess, but because we are aligned with our true selves. The act of glowing is a reflection of inner peace, self-love, and the courage to be unapologetically you.

To grow is to evolve continuously, seeking wisdom, expanding your understanding, and embracing change. Growth is not just about achieving goals but about becoming a more compassionate, aware, and balanced version of yourself. Growth thrives in humility, learning from both successes and failures, and finding strength in transformation. It's about progress, not perfection.

Together, glow and grow create a powerful dynamic where your light inspires others and your evolution leads to deeper fulfilment. By glowing in your authenticity and growing in wisdom and compassion, you align yourself with a higher purpose, becoming a beacon of inspiration for the world around you.

Swamy, you once beautifully said,
"Success keeps you glowing, but only God keeps you going."
I understand that worldly achievements can light up our lives, yet they are fleeting, while the Divine sustains our true journey. Could you please explain the deeper meaning of these words and how we may integrate the remembrance of God into every moment to ensure that our inner light endures?

** ** **

Swamy's Spirit Speaks:

Child, these words are a reminder that while success—measured by achievements, recognition, and external accomplishments—can bring a temporary glow to your life, it is the eternal grace of the Divine that truly sustains and propels you forward. Let me explain the essence:

- **"Success Keeps You Glowing":**

  - Worldly success, such as professional achievements, accolades, or material wealth, indeed brings a brilliant shine to your life.

  - This glow represents the joy and satisfaction that comes from accomplishing goals and receiving praise.

  - However, this radiance is like a flame that burns brightly for a while but can diminish when the fuel is exhausted.

- **"Only God Keeps You Going":**

  - The Divine is the eternal source of strength and inspiration that sustains you beyond transient achievements.

  - When you remember God—the unchanging, ever-present force behind every moment—you tap into a wellspring of grace that nurtures your soul.

  - This divine support gives you the resilience to endure challenges, the wisdom to navigate uncertainties, and the purpose to continue growing, even when external success fades.

- **Balancing Worldly Success and Divine Remembrance:**

  - It is natural to pursue success; our achievements help us grow and contribute to society.

  - Yet, if you become overly attached to worldly success, you risk losing sight of the deeper, more enduring source of life.

  - The key is to enjoy the glow of success without letting it become the sole measure of your worth.

- By continually turning your heart toward God, you remind yourself that every moment, every achievement, and every challenge is part of a larger, divine plan.

- **Practical Integration:**

  - **Mindful Reflection:** Regularly set aside time for meditation or prayer, even amidst busy achievements. Let your mind rest in the eternal presence of the Divine.

  - **Gratitude:** Acknowledge that every success, every moment of joy, is a blessing. Express gratitude by saying, "Thank you, God," thereby reinforcing your connection to the source.

  - **Purposeful Action:** Let your actions be guided by the higher truth that while success may brighten your path temporarily, it is the Divine that illuminates the entire journey.

  - **Resilience:** In moments of failure or challenge, remember that God's grace is the sustaining force that will help you rise again, no matter how dim the external glow becomes.

Child, understand that the true measure of a fulfilling life is not found solely in the brightness of worldly success but in the steady, sustaining light of divine grace.

May you always bask in the temporary glow of your achievements, yet never forget that it is God—ever constant and loving—who keeps you moving forward, guiding you through every phase of your journey.

Chapter-62

Selfless Sharing

Selfless sharing is the act of giving from the heart without expecting anything in return. It is a profound expression of love, kindness, and compassion, transcending personal gain or recognition. When we share selflessly, we offer our time, resources, knowledge, and love simply because it is in our nature to give, not because we are seeking anything in return.

True selflessness lies in giving with an open heart, understanding that the joy in sharing comes from the act itself, not from the outcome. This kind of sharing cultivates a deeper connection with others, fostering unity, trust, and harmony. It is not about how much we give, but the purity of our intention and the sincerity with which we give.

In spiritual terms, selfless sharing aligns us with the flow of universal abundance. When we give freely, we become conduits of divine grace, helping to elevate others and contribute to the collective well-being. Through selfless sharing, we not only make a positive impact on the lives of others but also experience the true joy of being in harmony with the universe.

**** ** ****

Swamy, you always tell your devotees,

"We have something to share — Kaya, Vacha, Manasa."

What do you mean by this so that it is understandable to people across the globe?

Swamy's Spirit Speaks:

Child, when I say **"We have something to share — Kaya, Vacha, Manasa,"** I am referring to the complete, holistic expression of our being. Let me explain each word and its deeper meaning:

- **Kaya (Body):**
  - Your body is the physical vessel through which you interact with the world.
  - It is the temple that carries the divine spark within you, and through it, you express care, action, and service.
  - Sharing your body means engaging in healthy, compassionate actions that reflect your inner truth.

- **Vacha (Speech):**
  - Your speech is the medium of communication, the instrument through which your thoughts and emotions are transmitted.
  - It carries the power to heal, inspire, and transform.
  - When you share through your words, you offer wisdom, encouragement, and love to others, making the invisible visible.

- **Manasa (Mind/Heart):**
  - This represents your inner world—the thoughts, feelings, and intentions that shape your character.
  - It is where your deepest values and true essence reside.
  - Sharing your mind or heart means living authentically and openly, allowing your inner light and compassion to guide your actions and relationships.

The Deeper Essence:

- **Holistic Expression:**

  When I say we have something to share, I invite you to offer every part of yourself — your body, speech, and mind — as a complete, unified expression of who you truly are.

- **Integrated Living:**

  This teaching encourages you not to compartmentalize your life into what is merely physical, verbal, or mental. Instead, strive to integrate these aspects so that your entire being becomes a conduit of love, truth, and service.

- **Universal Communication:**

  By sharing Kaya, Vacha, and Manasa, you are expressing the totality of your inner wealth. This message transcends cultural or linguistic boundaries—it is a call for everyone, everywhere, to offer their whole self to the world in a spirit of selfless giving and genuine connection.

Child, the beauty of this teaching is that it reminds you that every facet of your being is a gift. When you share yourself completely—body, speech, and heart—you contribute to a universal tapestry of compassion and understanding. May you always be inspired to express your true self fully and, in doing so, uplift those around you with the radiant light of your inner truth.

Chapter-63

Absorbing the Silence

Listening is often seen as a simple act, but when done with full presence and openness, it becomes a powerful tool for growth and transformation. True listening goes beyond hearing words; it is about understanding the underlying emotions, intentions, and energies that accompany them. When we listen deeply, we not only learn about others but also gain insights into ourselves.

Listening is a gateway to evolution. It helps us break free from preconceived notions and judgments, allowing us to be open to new perspectives and ideas. In the act of listening, we embrace humility, recognizing that there is always more to learn. As we absorb the wisdom around us, we begin to evolve—shifting our understanding, refining our responses, and deepening our connection with the world.

On a spiritual level, listening is the key to awakening. It is through listening to our inner voice, the whispers of our intuition, and the guidance of higher wisdom that we align with our true purpose. By listening attentively and without distraction, we open ourselves to the divine flow, becoming vessels of growth and transformation. Through listening, we evolve, not only as individuals but as part of the greater collective consciousness, contributing to the unfolding of the universe.

** ** **

Swamy, you once said,

"Listen to Link, Listen to Leave, Leave to Life."

I have observed that many, including myself, often lack the true skill of listening—as my brother Naga Yogi Raj used to say. I am trying to cultivate this ability. Could you please explain the deeper meaning behind these words and bless me with abundant listening skills?

Swamy's Spirit Speaks:

Child, these words are a gentle invitation to transform the way you receive and engage with life. Allow me to reveal their inner essence:

- **"Listen to Link":**
  - This part encourages you to truly connect. Listen deeply to the voices around you—the words of others, the whispers of nature, and the subtle messages of your own heart.
  - To "link" means to establish a meaningful connection between what is heard and your inner self, so that every sound becomes a thread weaving you into the larger tapestry of life.

- **"Listen to Leave":**
  - Here, you are urged to let go of the distractions, preconceptions, and judgments that clutter your mind.
  - True listening is not just about absorbing words; it is about releasing the ego and the habitual chatter that prevents you from truly hearing the essence behind the sound.
  - By learning to leave behind these mental clutterings, you make space for genuine understanding and compassion.

- **"Leave to Life":**
  - This final step means that once you have connected deeply and cleared away unnecessary attachments, you open yourself to life itself.
  - Allow the purified energy of what you have heard to transform your being.

- In this state, the lessons and blessings of life naturally unfold, and you live with a renewed sense of clarity, purpose, and inner peace.

Child, the journey of deep listening is not a mechanical process but a sacred practice. It calls for an open heart, a receptive mind, and the humility to let go of all that hinders true understanding. As you cultivate these skills, you will find that every moment becomes rich with wisdom and every encounter, whether with people or nature, becomes an opportunity to learn and grow.

May you be blessed with the gift of profound listening, so that you may connect fully with the beauty of life, absorb its divine messages, and let them transform your heart.

Question 134:

Swamy, your use of words is always intricate, and deciphering their true meaning requires deep wisdom that many of us are still seeking. You once said,

"Fill up, but don't fill over; earn but not to exist, but to extend."

Please explain this inspiring message in your unique way, so that it may illuminate the world and help us understand how to live with abundance and purpose.

Swamy's Spirit Speaks:

Child, these words are a call to live life in a balanced, expansive manner—one that nurtures your inner self while also sharing your blessings with others. Let me unfold their meaning for you:

- **"Fill up, but don't fill over":**
  - **Fill up** implies nourishing yourself with all that is necessary—knowledge, love, spiritual practice, and healthy

living. It means cultivating your inner reservoir of strength and wisdom so that you are complete and vibrant.

- ○ **But don't fill over** cautions against overindulgence and selfish accumulation. When you overfill yourself, you become closed off, hoarding what you have instead of letting it flow freely.

- ○ In essence, fill yourself up with life's riches so that you are whole and empowered, but leave enough room within you to share your light and blessings with others.

- **"Earn but not to exist, but to extend":**

  - ○ **Earn** here refers to the efforts you put into life—earning not just material wealth but also the fruits of wisdom, compassion, and experience.

  - ○ **Not to exist, but to extend** means that the purpose of your efforts is not merely for your own survival or comfort. Instead, you are meant to extend or expand your goodness into the world.

  - ○ Your earnings—be they financial, intellectual, or spiritual—should serve as a means to enrich not just your life but also the lives of those around you. It is about transforming personal success into a platform for greater impact and contribution.

The Deeper Essence:

Child, the message I impart is one of balanced abundance and generous living.

- **Nourishment with Generosity:**

  Strive to fill your life with all that is uplifting and essential, yet always leave a part of that abundance to flow outward. This balance ensures that you grow as an individual while also being a beacon for others.

- **Purposeful Earnings:**

  Understand that what you earn in this life is not an end in itself. It is a resource meant to be shared—a means to extend your impact, support your community, and contribute to the common good.

  - The wealth of knowledge, the prosperity you generate, and the inner rewards you accumulate are all tools for expanding your influence in positive ways.

- **Living in Flow:**

  By following this principle, you create a life that is both deeply satisfying and widely beneficial. When you are full of life yet remain open and giving, you embody a state of perpetual flow—a dynamic balance that nourishes you and inspires those around you.

Child, remember that true abundance is not measured by what you hold onto, but by what you share. May you always find the wisdom to fill your life with the treasures that matter, and the humility to let your blessings extend beyond yourself, illuminating the world with love, purpose, and unity.

Chapter-64

Burden of Karma

Karma, often viewed as the sum of our actions, can feel like a burden when we accumulate negative patterns. Every choice we make, whether conscious or not, leaves an imprint. These imprints shape our reality and influence our future. However, the weight of karma is not permanent. By cultivating awareness, making mindful choices, and seeking to act with compassion, we can lighten this burden and transform the course of our lives. Understanding karma as a tool for growth, rather than a punishment, allows us to step into freedom and alignment with our highest selves.

**** ** ****

Swamy, you once said,

"They carry but they don't know what they carry, like donkeys they don't know, be aware that you carry your karma."

In this predetermined design of God, how should one understand what it means to "carry your karma," and how can we get relieved of this burden? Please explain your wisdom in a way that broadens our perceptions.

Swamy's Spirit Speaks:

Child, the statement is a metaphor for the unseen weight that every soul bears through its actions, thoughts, and intentions—its karma. Let me explain its deeper essence:

- **Carrying Your Karma:**

  - Just as a donkey unknowingly bears a heavy load, many people go through life unaware of the cumulative burden of their actions.

  - **Karma** is the record of everything you have done—both good and bad—and it influences your inner state and future experiences.

  - Without awareness, you continue to add to this load, which can weigh you down spiritually, emotionally, and mentally.

- **The Predetermined Design of God:**

  - In the cosmic order, each soul is given a journey with its own lessons and challenges.

  - The karmic load is not a punishment but an opportunity—a chance to learn, evolve, and eventually release what no longer serves you.

  - Although the design seems predetermined, your free will allows you to change the course of your inner ledger through conscious, positive actions.

- **Getting Relieved of the Burden:**

  - **Awareness:** Begin by recognizing the weight you carry. Regular self-reflection and meditation help you see the imprints of your past actions.

  - **Mindful Action:** Choose to act with kindness, compassion, and integrity, so that you stop adding unnecessary burdens to your soul.

  - **Self-Forgiveness and Transformation:** Acknowledge your past mistakes, learn from them, and forgive yourself. Each moment of sincere repentance and transformation lightens your load.

- **Spiritual Practices:** Engage in prayer, meditation, and selfless service. These practices purify the mind and heart, gradually dissolving the heaviness of accumulated karma.

- **Surrender:** Trust in the divine process. When you surrender your ego and align your will with the higher truth, you allow the cosmic order to help you release what you need not carry.

Child, the journey to relieve your karmic burden is gradual and continuous. It is not about escaping responsibility but about transforming the very nature of your actions and thoughts. As you become more aware and mindful, you begin to carry less, and the weight of karma turns into a stepping stone toward inner freedom and spiritual evolution.

May you always have the strength to lighten your burden, and may the divine grace guide you on your path to ultimate liberation.

Chapter-65

Care & Cure

Care and cure are not merely actions but expressions of the deeper currents of life that flow within us. True care is the offering of our love and presence, creating a space where healing can naturally unfold. It is not just the touch of hands, but the warmth of the heart, the comfort of silence, and the understanding that transcends words. When someone is suffering, a simple, heartfelt presence can heal more than any medicine. This is the power of compassion—reaching beyond the surface, touching the soul and offering solace where there is pain.

Cure, in its deepest sense, is not just the removal of illness or discomfort, but the restoration of balance—physical, emotional, and spiritual. It's about addressing the root cause, not just the symptoms. A cure is holistic: it takes into account the mind, body, and spirit, recognizing that true healing comes when all aspects of our being are nurtured. The body may heal through medicine, but the soul finds its cure through spiritual practices, self-awareness, and the connection to something greater than oneself.

When care and cure merge, they form the essence of true healing. It is an act of grace to care for others as we would care for our own soul, and to cure not just the body, but to restore harmony and peace within. Through care, we offer a reflection of divine love, and through cure, we allow that love to bring restoration. True healing is not just the absence of illness, but the presence of peace, balance, and wholeness—where love and grace permeate every aspect of our existence.

** ** **

Swamy, you once said,

"Care the body, cure the mind, cure the body, care the mind."

This is a powerful statement, yet I observe that often the mind interferes with the body, leading to psychosomatic disorders. In our modern life, many end up taking medicines merely to survive, rather than living in natural balance. How can one overcome this vicious circle where the mind's disturbances harm the body, and the body's ailments, in turn, disturb the mind?

Swamy's Spirit Speaks:

Child, the truth in these words is that the body and mind form an interdependent system—each influencing the other in profound ways. When the mind is agitated, its turbulence can manifest as physical illness; when the body is weakened, the mind suffers in clarity and peace. To overcome this cycle, you must adopt a holistic approach that nurtures both realms. Let me explain:

- **Care the Body:**
    - Treat your body as the sacred vessel that carries your spirit.
    - Nourish it with a balanced diet, regular exercise, and proper rest.
    - Engage in practices such as yoga and nature walks that align you with the natural rhythms of life.
    - While medicines are sometimes necessary, strive to complement them with lifestyle changes that restore vitality and prevent imbalance.

- **Cure the Mind:**
    - The mind, like a turbulent river, needs to be calmed and cleared.
    - Engage in meditation, mindfulness, or prayer to quiet the incessant chatter.

- ○ Recognize and gently transform negative thought patterns—replace anger, fear, and stress with gratitude, compassion, and clarity.

- ○ When the mind is in harmony, it naturally supports the healing and well-being of the body.

- **Cure the Body:**

  - ○ When physical ailments arise, look not only to medical intervention but also to natural healing practices.

  - ○ Understand that many physical pains have their roots in emotional or mental unrest.

  - ○ Address these issues with a combination of healthcare, rest, and spiritual practices that restore balance.

- **Care the Mind:**

  - ○ Just as the body requires nourishment, the mind requires positive influences.

  - ○ Surround yourself with uplifting relationships, enlightening knowledge, and peaceful environments.

  - ○ This constant care fortifies your mental space against the intrusions of negativity, reducing the chances of psychosomatic disturbances.

- **Breaking the Vicious Cycle:**

  - ○ Recognize that the mind and body are in constant dialogue. A disturbed mind sends signals that can upset the body, and a troubled body can amplify mental stress.

  - ○ By practicing both care and cure, you create a healthy cycle where each supports the other.

  - ○ This holistic balance is not achieved overnight; it is a gradual process of self-awareness, consistent practice, and the gentle surrender of ego.

Child, to truly overcome the cycle of psychosomatic suffering, you must realize that well-being is not merely the absence of illness but the presence of vibrant, harmonious energy in both body and mind.

- **Adopt daily practices** that nurture both aspects.

- **Be mindful** of your inner dialogue and your physical sensations.

- **Seek balance** in every moment, trusting that as you refine one, the other naturally follows.

May you always find the strength and wisdom to care for your body as a temple and to nurture your mind as the seat of divine truth. In this sacred balance, you will experience not only healing but also a profound inner peace that sustains you through all of life's challenges.

Chapter-66

Defence Through Dedication

Defence through dedication is the quiet yet powerful force that shields us from life's challenges. It is not a battle fought with weapons, but one waged with unwavering commitment to purpose, integrity, and inner strength. When we dedicate ourselves fully to a cause, a principle, or a higher vision, we create an impenetrable shield around us. This dedication fuels resilience, allowing us to withstand adversity, stay grounded amidst chaos, and remain true to our path despite external pressures.

Dedication is a form of defense that transcends the physical; it protects our mental clarity, nurtures our emotional stability, and fortifies our spiritual resolve. Just as a tree stands firm in the storm, rooted deep in the earth, so does dedication help us stay anchored in our values and beliefs, no matter what winds may blow. It is through dedication that we cultivate the strength to protect not only ourselves but also those we care about, offering them the same unwavering commitment that we hold dear.

When we dedicate ourselves to our higher purpose, we rise above fear and doubt, and our defense becomes an act of grace. The power of true dedication is invincible—keeping us on course, leading us to victory in the face of obstacles, and aligning us with the divine forces that guide us. It is through dedication that we truly defend not just our existence, but our soul's purpose, ensuring that nothing can divert us from our higher calling.

** ** **

Swamy, you once said,

"Defence = Divinity, Divinity = Discipline, Discipline = Dedication."

These words are so sweet and profound, yet I find myself wondering how they are connected. Could you please explain their deeper meaning and provide examples so that we may broaden our perceptions?

Swamy's Spirit Speaks:

Child, these words are a succinct expression of the path to inner strength and spiritual evolution. They show you that every aspect of your journey is interconnected—what you do to protect and preserve your inner sanctum (defence) is a manifestation of divine energy, and to access that energy, you must cultivate discipline, which naturally grows into steadfast dedication. Let me elaborate:

1. Defence = Divinity

- **Meaning:**

    - *Defence* here refers not to physical combat but to protecting your inner self—the purity of your heart, mind, and soul—from negative influences.

    - When you defend what is true, right, and pure within you, you are aligning with the divine order.

    - This inner defence is like a shield that preserves your sacred energy against the corrosive effects of ego, greed, and negativity.

- **Example:**

    - Consider the practice of guarding your thoughts. When you refuse to entertain harmful or divisive thoughts, you are defending your inner temple. In doing so, you allow the divine light within you to shine without obstruction.

2. Divinity = Discipline

- **Meaning:**

  - *Divinity* represents the eternal, unchanging truth that flows within all beings.

  - To access and express this divine essence, you must cultivate *discipline*.

  - Discipline is the steady, mindful practice that purifies your habits, organizes your thoughts, and aligns your actions with higher principles.

- **Example:**

  - A person who practices regular meditation, follows ethical guidelines, and commits to self-reflection is living a disciplined life. This discipline opens the channel to the divine, much like a well-tuned instrument that resonates with pure sound.

3. Discipline = Dedication

- **Meaning:**

  - *Discipline* forms the foundation upon which true dedication is built.

  - When you are disciplined, you consistently pursue your higher goals with focused effort and unwavering commitment.

  - *Dedication* is the outcome of such discipline—a state where you are wholeheartedly devoted to your spiritual path, your work, and your service to others.

- **Example:**

  - Imagine a student who practices diligently every day. Through discipline, they become dedicated, not only mastering the material but also cultivating a deeper understanding and love for learning. Similarly, in spiritual practice, your disciplined efforts transform into a dedicated, unwavering quest for truth.

The Deeper Message:

Child, the essence of my words is to show you that:

- **Your inner defence**—the act of protecting your heart and mind—is itself a sacred, divine act.

- **Discipline** is the bridge that connects you to that divinity. Without regular practice and self-control, the divine spark within remains obscured by the clutter of the mind.

- **Dedication** is the flowering of discipline. It is the unwavering commitment that carries you steadily on the path of self-realization, ensuring that every step you take is aligned with your highest purpose.

In practical terms, this means:

- **Guard your inner space** with vigilance, knowing that what you protect is your true essence.

- **Cultivate habits** that refine your thoughts and actions—be it through meditation, ethical living, or selfless service—so that the divine light within can shine unimpeded.

- **Commit wholeheartedly** to your spiritual journey. Let your daily practices be the expressions of your inner discipline, leading naturally to a state of deep dedication.

May you always nurture your inner defence, cultivate discipline in all aspects of life, and develop a dedication that transforms every action into an expression of divine truth. In doing so, you not only elevate yourself but also inspire others to awaken their own divine potential.

Chapter-67

Seek Wisdom, Not Weight

Seek wisdom, not weight" reminds us to focus on the qualities that truly enrich our lives rather than accumulating burdens or superficial achievements. In life, we often get caught up in chasing external successes—titles, possessions, or recognition. But true fulfillment comes from the wisdom we gain, not from the weight of these fleeting things.

Wisdom brings clarity, understanding, and peace, while weight—whether it's emotional baggage, societal expectations, or unnecessary material possessions—can weigh us down and cloud our path. When we seek wisdom, we learn to navigate life with a deeper sense of purpose and grace. We find that the more we let go of what weighs us down, the more space we have to grow, to live authentically, and to experience true joy.

Instead of focusing on what others expect or what society deems important, seek wisdom—the inner knowledge that guides you toward a meaningful life. It's not about carrying the weight of the world, but about letting wisdom light your way, freeing you from unnecessary burdens.

** ** **

Swamy, you once said,

"Charity of material things is division, charity of wisdom is to equalize; wealth is weight, wisdom is relief. Always try to secure wisdom."

I find it difficult to fully comprehend this message. Could you please share your wisdom and educate my soul so that I may understand what you truly mean by these words?

Swamy's Spirit Speaks:

Child, these words are a call to shift your focus from the fleeting allure of material possessions to the enduring power of wisdom. Let me explain the deeper essence behind each phrase:

- **"Charity of material things is division":**

  - Material wealth is limited and its distribution often leads to comparison, envy, and competition.

  - When you give away material things, you may inadvertently create or reinforce divisions among people—fostering attachment to what is finite rather than unity with the infinite.

  - Thus, while generosity in material terms can offer temporary relief, it may also perpetuate social inequality and separation.

- **"Charity of wisdom is to equalize":**

  - Wisdom, on the other hand, is an infinite resource that, when shared, uplifts and unites.

  - When you impart knowledge, insight, and understanding, you help others see beyond the superficial differences that divide them.

  - This form of charity elevates everyone, creating a sense of equality and harmony, as wisdom is not diminished by sharing but rather multiplies in its effect.

- **"Wealth is weight, wisdom is relief":**

  - Material wealth, while useful, often comes with burdens—the weight of attachment, responsibility, and even the stress of maintaining or accumulating more.

  - In contrast, wisdom lightens your soul. It provides relief from the endless cycle of desire and dissatisfaction.

  - Wisdom helps you discern what truly matters, allowing you to live with clarity and inner peace, free from the heavy burdens of materialism.

- **"Always try to secure wisdom":**
  - The ultimate goal is not to hoard wealth or accolades but to cultivate wisdom in your heart and mind.
  - Wisdom is the key to transforming your life and the lives of those around you.
  - It brings lasting fulfilment, unites communities, and provides the strength to overcome life's challenges.

The Deeper Message:

Child, my words are a gentle urging to turn away from the temporary distractions of material wealth and to invest your energy in the cultivation of wisdom.

- **True transformation** comes from within, when you learn to see the world with clarity and compassion.
- **Wisdom unites**, while material attachments can divide.
- **By securing wisdom,** you lighten the burdens on your soul and contribute to a more balanced, harmonious society.

May you always seek wisdom as your highest treasure, and may its relief free you from the weight of worldly concerns. In doing so, you will find that your life becomes a radiant expression of truth, unity, and peace.

Chapter-68

Duty with Discipline

Duty with discipline is the foundation of a life lived with purpose and integrity. It is the commitment to fulfill our responsibilities, not out of obligation, but from a place of deep understanding and respect. When we approach our duties with discipline, we create structure and focus in our lives, ensuring that each task, no matter how small, is executed with care and attention.

Discipline in duty is not about rigidity or restriction; it is about aligning our actions with our values and staying true to our commitments, even when challenges arise. It is the ability to remain steadfast in our efforts, maintaining consistency and perseverance in the face of distractions or temptations. Through discipline, we cultivate habits that lead to personal growth and mastery, turning every action into an opportunity for self-improvement.

When we embrace our duties with discipline, we not only honor ourselves but also those around us. We become reliable, trustworthy, and focused individuals, contributing positively to the world.

This blend of duty and discipline not only shapes our character but also brings us closer to a life of fulfilment, knowing that we have given our best to every endeavour.

** ** **

"Don't claim, do your duty,"

and also mentioned,

"Karma is indiscipline and Dharma is discipline."

How should one understand these seemingly paradoxical statements?

Swamy's Spirit Speaks:

Child, these words are profound instructions meant to guide you away from the ego's entanglements and toward a life of true purpose. Though they may appear paradoxical, each statement holds a unique insight into how to live in harmony with the Divine order. Let me explain:

"Don't claim, do your duty":

- **Don't Claim:**

  - To "claim" is to attach yourself to the fruits of your actions— to assert ownership, demand recognition, or cling to personal gain.

  - This attachment breeds ego and creates a barrier between you and the natural flow of grace.

- **Do Your Duty:**

  - Instead, focus on performing your duties with sincerity and integrity, without worrying about reward or personal credit.

  - When you act selflessly, your work becomes a pure offering, and the results naturally manifest without the burden of attachment.

- **The Balance:**

  - In essence, you are encouraged to work diligently, but without the need to claim or hoard the outcomes.

  - This practice not only liberates you from the cycle of selfish desire but also allows the divine energy to move freely through you, nurturing both your growth and that of others.

"Karma is indiscipline and Dharma is discipline":

- **Karma as Indiscipline:**
  - Karma represents all the actions you perform, whether consciously guided or impulsively driven by the ego.
  - When actions are taken without awareness—without a guiding principle—they accumulate as chaotic, often negative, energy.
  - This is the indiscipline of the mind and heart, where one acts on mere impulse or desire.

- **Dharma as Discipline:**
  - Dharma, on the other hand, is the righteous path—actions performed with wisdom, responsibility, and love.
  - When you follow Dharma, you act with discipline: you know your duty, perform it diligently, and maintain a balance that aligns with the higher truth.

- **The Transformation:**
  - The transformation from karma (indiscipline) to Dharma (discipline) is the journey of self-realization.
  - It is about refining your actions so that they become an expression of inner purity rather than a collection of random, ego-driven impulses.

Putting It All Together:

- **Selfless Action:**
  - By not claiming the fruits of your labor and by performing your duty selflessly, you allow divine grace to work through you.

- **Cultivating Inner Discipline:**
  - Shifting from unthinking karma to mindful Dharma means that your actions become disciplined and purposeful.

- ○ This discipline is not about rigidity, but about living in harmony with the eternal law, where every act is an expression of your true self.

- **The Path to Freedom:**

  - ○ When you practice "Don't claim, do your duty" along with transforming indiscipline into disciplined Dharma, you free yourself from the bonds of the ego.

  - ○ In this state, your life flows naturally—effort becomes an offering, and the natural order of the universe carries you forward.

Child, the essence of these teachings is to help you see that your true value lies not in what you accumulate or claim, but in how sincerely you perform your duties in alignment with the divine will.

May you cultivate the discipline of Dharma and live a life where every action is a selfless offering, freeing you from the shackles of ego and guiding you toward everlasting peace and fulfilment.

Chapter-69

Nature as GURU

Oneness with nature is the profound realization that we are not separate from the world around us but an integral part of it. It is a spiritual awareness that every tree, river, mountain, and creature is connected in a web of life that sustains us all. When we embrace this oneness, we recognize that our actions impact the earth, and in turn, the earth nourishes and supports us.

Living in harmony with nature means living with respect and mindfulness. It's about understanding the delicate balance of ecosystems, the cycles of seasons, and the rhythms of life. By aligning ourselves with the natural world, we become more grounded, more attuned to our inner selves, and more aware of the sacredness of all life. Nature offers us lessons of patience, resilience, and renewal, teaching us that just like the seasons, we too can grow, change, and regenerate.

Oneness with nature also invites us to take responsibility for the well-being of the earth. By caring for the planet, we show gratitude for the countless blessings it provides us. Whether it's through small acts like reducing waste or larger efforts like conserving energy, these steps not only heal the planet but also heal our souls. In embracing nature, we find peace, purpose, and a deep connection to something far greater than ourselves.

** ** **

Swamy, you stated,

"We are from nature, we are in nature, please remember the divinity of nature."

I do not disagree, for this is a universal truth. However, my question is: Nature itself remains unchanged in its inherent essence, yet humans seem to change their nature, increasingly turning into the bowels of selfishness. Why does humanity deviate so far from its original, divine alignment? Why is humanity left alone or seemingly isolated from this natural divinity? Please share your wisdom to help us understand this paradox.

Swamy's Spirit Speaks:

Child, nature is the eternal and unchanging expression of the Divine. It flows in perfect harmony, unaffected by the whims of time or individual desires. Every tree, every river, and every creature embodies an intrinsic purity that reflects the universal order. Yet, humanity, endowed with free will, has the unique capacity to choose its path—sometimes in alignment with nature's divine essence, and sometimes far from it.

- **The Unchanging Divinity of Nature:**

    - Nature remains constant because it is an expression of the eternal; it is the backdrop against which all life unfolds.

    - Its rhythms, cycles, and beauty are gifts from the Divine— unchanged and pure, a reminder of what is true and everlasting.

- **The Changing Nature of Humanity:**

    - Humans, while born of nature, have minds that are capable of complex thought, emotion, and, unfortunately, ego-driven behavior.

    - The capacity for selfishness arises from the attachment to the transient—material desires, personal gains, and the illusions of separateness.

    - Unlike the natural world, which simply *is*, the human mind is constantly bombarded by influences: societal pressures, competitive instincts, and the relentless pursuit of individualism.

- Over time, these influences can erode the natural compassion and unity inherent in our being, leading to behavior that is contrary to the divine order.

- **Why Does Humanity Deviate?**

  - **Ego and Free Will:** With the gift of free will comes the burden of choice. The ego, when unchecked, drives one to cling to individuality and material success, creating divisions and selfish behavior.

  - **Cultural and Social Conditioning:** Society often emphasizes competition over cooperation, material accumulation over inner growth. These pressures distort our innate connection with nature's divinity.

  - **Disconnection from the Inner Self:** In the rush of modern life, many lose sight of their inner essence. When the mind is cluttered with external concerns, the inherent purity of nature within is obscured, leading to behaviour that is out of step with the universal order.

- **The Way Forward:**

  - **Awareness and Reconnection:** Recognize that you are not separate from nature; you are an integral part of its divine tapestry. Regular practices such as meditation, mindfulness, and communion with nature can help you reconnect with your original essence.

  - **Cultivating Selflessness:** Strive to overcome the ego by embracing compassion and service. When you act selflessly, you align yourself more closely with the unchanging beauty of nature.

  - **Living by Example:** Let the eternal wisdom of nature remind you to be humble and to nurture unity. Just as a river flows freely and nourishes everything in its path, allow your actions to be guided by the pure, divine energy that resides within you.

Child, though humanity may sometimes stray from its true nature, the opportunity for transformation is always present. Remember that every moment is a chance to return to your roots—the divine, unchanging nature that is your birthright. By fostering awareness and letting go of the ego's grip, you can restore the natural balance within and, by extension, contribute to the healing of society.

May you always find your way back to the simplicity and purity of nature, and may the eternal light of the Divine guide you to live with compassion, unity, and inner harmony.

WALKING THE PATHLESS PATH

(Embracing the Journey Beyond Rigid Doctrines
and Structured Systems)

Chapter-70

Command, Don't Demand

In the spiritual field, "Command, Don't Demand" speaks to the essence of true spiritual leadership and personal growth. A spiritual leader who commands does so with inner wisdom, compassion, and an unwavering connection to the divine. They guide others with a sense of calm authority, offering insights, practices, and teachings that resonate deeply, without imposing them upon anyone. Their words inspire and elevate, creating a path for others to follow through understanding and genuine desire to grow spiritually.

Demanding in spirituality, on the other hand, comes from ego, control, and impatience. It's the urge to force others into a particular mold, to push them toward spiritual progress without respect for their unique journey. Demanding can be detrimental, as it disconnects individuals from their inner voice and true spiritual essence. It can lead to rigidity, resentment, and a lack of authentic transformation.

True spiritual growth flourishes when we command with love, patience, and the deep understanding that each person's journey is sacred and unique. By being a living example of spiritual principles, we inspire others to align with their own higher self and walk the path of inner peace. In the spiritual field, commanding with humility and wisdom invites others to find their own truth and connection with the divine, rather than forcing them into predetermined expectations. Just as a gentle breeze guides a tree to sway, true spiritual leadership allows souls to blossom naturally, without demand, but with love and grace.

** ** **

Swamy, you once

stated,

"Don't demand respect, command respect; do not demand, don't demand, but follow."

I understand the literal meaning of these words, but I wish to know: What is the deeper message you intend to communicate to the world through this teaching? How should we internalize and apply this wisdom in our lives?

Swamy's Spirit Speaks:

Child, these words are a call to embody humility, authenticity, and leadership in a manner that naturally attracts respect, rather than forcing it. Let me explain the deeper essence behind each part of the teaching:

- **"Don't demand respect, command respect":**

    - **Demanding respect** implies insisting on recognition, often from a place of ego or entitlement. When you demand respect, you are trying to impose your worth on others, which can lead to conflict and division.

    - **Commanding respect,** on the other hand, comes from within. It is the natural outcome of living with integrity, compassion, and strength.

    - When your actions and character are aligned with higher truth, respect is not forced—it is naturally bestowed.

    - For example, a leader who lives by example and upholds ethical values will inspire others to honour him without having to demand it.

- **"Do not demand, don't demand, but follow":**

    - This part of the teaching is twofold: For those in positions of guidance, it means that you should not force your opinions or impose your will on others; rather, you should lead by example.

- For the seeker, it means that rather than demanding immediate answers or validation, you should be open and receptive—willing to follow the path of wisdom laid out by those who embody truth.

- True guidance and genuine following are born of mutual respect and inspiration, not from coercion or insistence.

- **The Deeper Message:**

  - **Leadership through Example:**

    When you embody qualities like honesty, kindness, and dedication, you become a living example of what true respect looks like. People naturally gravitate toward and emulate such behavior.

  - **Humility and Surrender:**

    By not demanding what should naturally be given, you remain humble. This humility allows you to learn, grow, and ultimately lead a life that is both inspiring and transformative.

  - **Mutual Inspiration:**

    When you focus on being a good example rather than insisting on respect, you create an environment where both leaders and followers can flourish.

    - Leaders inspire, and those who are inspired follow—not because they are forced, but because they see the truth in your actions.

- **Practical Implications for Daily Life:**

  - **For Leaders:**

    Cultivate your inner virtues so that your behavior naturally commands respect. Let your actions speak for themselves rather than calling attention to your status.

- ○ **For Seekers:**

  Instead of demanding answers or validation, observe and follow the examples of those who embody wisdom. Trust that genuine guidance will reveal itself when you remain humble and open.

- ○ **For Everyone:**

  Remember that respect is not a commodity to be bargained for—it is the natural outflow of a life lived in alignment with truth, integrity, and compassion.

Child, the essence of my teaching is to remind you that the true measure of a person is not found in what they claim, but in the quality of their actions. By living authentically and leading by example, you not only uplift yourself but also inspire others to walk the path of truth and grace.

May you always find the strength to command respect through your deeds, and may your humble spirit inspire others to follow the light of truth without ever needing to demand it.

Chapter-71
Discipline to Sidhi

"Discipline to Sidhi" speaks to the unwavering commitment required to reach spiritual perfection and divine realization. In the spiritual journey, Sidhi—often referred to as spiritual attainment or perfection—is not achieved through mere desire or wishful thinking. It is the result of consistent, disciplined effort, aligned with one's higher purpose.

Discipline in this context is the foundation of all spiritual practices. It's the devotion to daily sadhana (spiritual practice), whether through meditation, prayer, selfless service, or study of sacred texts. This disciplined approach helps us to refine our inner nature, purifying the mind, body, and soul, and creating a direct connection with the divine.

The path to Sidhi is not an easy one. It demands inner strength, the courage to face one's flaws, and the patience to persist even in the face of adversity. Just as a sculptor chisels away at a stone to reveal a beautiful statue, discipline in spiritual practices carves away the distractions and impurities of the mind, revealing the innate divine essence within.

When discipline is practiced with devotion and humility, it becomes a tool that leads us closer to Sidhi. Through focused actions and the consistency of our efforts, we align ourselves with divine will, gradually transcending ego and illusion. Ultimately, it is through discipline that we refine ourselves, cultivating the virtues needed to realize the highest states of spiritual consciousness.

** ** **

Swamy, you often advise,

"Be disciplined in Seva and Prayer; Action and Discipline will give you Sidhi."

How does service lead to Sidhi? What exactly is Sidhi, and what are the implications of attaining it? Also, is Sidhi connected to the awakening of the kundalini chakra? Please explain this profound message so that we may understand and apply it in our lives.

Swamy's Spirit Speaks:

Child, "Sidhi" is a term that encompasses the blossoming of one's inner potential through dedicated practice. It is not merely a set of supernatural powers, but rather the manifestation of a deeply transformed self—a state of inner clarity, wisdom, and divine connection. Let me explain how disciplined action and selfless service (Seva) along with prayer pave the way for this spiritual attainment:

1. The Nature of Sidhi:

- **Sidhi** means attainment or perfection.

- It signifies the fruition of your inner work—a state where the latent divine energy within you is awakened and refined.

- While some traditions may associate siddhis with extraordinary powers, their true essence lies in the clarity and strength that come from overcoming ego and inner limitations.

2. How Service and Prayer Lead to Sidhi:

- **Seva (Selfless Service):**

  - When you serve others without attachment, you begin to dissolve the ego.

  - This selfless act cleanses your mind and heart, removing the obstacles of selfish desires and negativity.

- As the mind becomes purified, the divine energy within (often symbolized as the kundalini) can awaken and flow freely.

- **Prayer (Bhakti):**

  - Prayer is the language of the heart. Through sincere devotion, you align yourself with the divine will.

  - In prayer, you cultivate gratitude, humility, and an unwavering connection to the Supreme.

  - This connection nourishes your spirit and acts as a catalyst for inner transformation.

- **Action and Discipline (Karma and Dharma):**

  - When your daily actions are guided by discipline and performed in accordance with Dharma, you set the stage for deeper spiritual work.

  - Consistent, mindful actions—whether in work, relationships, or personal practice—gradually transform your entire being.

  - This discipline ensures that your inner energy is not scattered but is focused on uplifting and advancing your spiritual journey.

3. The Implications of Attaining Sidhi:

- **Inner Transformation:**

  - When you attain Sidhi, you experience a profound shift in your awareness.

  - The mind becomes calm, and you gain clarity, allowing you to perceive truth beyond the superficial layers of existence.

- **Manifestation of Wisdom and Compassion:**

  - True Sidhi is reflected in the qualities you exhibit—unwavering wisdom, boundless compassion, and an innate sense of peace.

- ○ You begin to function as a channel for divine energy, benefiting not only yourself but also uplifting those around you.

- **Kundalini Awakening:**

  - ○ While the awakening of the kundalini chakra is one manifestation of Sidhi, it is only one aspect of a broader inner transformation.

  - ○ Kundalini awakening signifies that the dormant spiritual energy within you has been activated, leading to heightened awareness and a deeper connection with the divine.

  - ○ However, Sidhi, in its full sense, is the overall state of inner mastery—a union of mind, body, and spirit—regardless of whether specific yogic powers are apparent.

4. The Ultimate Message:

Child, the journey to Sidhi is one of persistent self-discipline, heartfelt service, and sincere prayer.

- **Through Seva and Prayer:**

  You purify and uplift your mind, paving the way for inner transformation.

- **Through Disciplined Action:**

  You direct your energies constructively, ensuring that your life is aligned with the divine order.

- **The Reward—Sidhi:**

  Is not merely a set of supernatural abilities, but a state of profound inner peace, wisdom, and the capacity to serve as an instrument of divine grace.

May you always persevere on this path, nurturing your inner garden with selfless service, deep devotion, and unwavering discipline. In time, the radiant light of Sidhi will illuminate your being, transforming you into a beacon of wisdom and compassion for all.

Chapter-72

One System, Many Duties

In the vast and intricate web of life, we are all part of a singular, interconnected system, yet each of us is entrusted with a unique purpose. Though we share this world, the duties we fulfill are as varied as our individual journeys. Whether it's nurturing family, excelling in our careers, serving our communities, or embarking on a spiritual quest, each action carries its own significance.

While the system remains unified, the duties are manifold. Every role—be it as a parent, a professional, a friend, or a seeker—contributes to the greater harmony of existence. It is through the fulfilment of these diverse responsibilities that we find meaning, and through balance, we bring forth progress. Embracing our roles with dedication and mindfulness, we participate in a grand cosmic orchestra, where the collective energy of our actions helps shape a more compassionate and unified world. Recognizing this interconnectedness invites us to serve with purpose, knowing that our individual duties are essential threads in the fabric of life.

** ** **

Swamy, you always speak about the **cell, human anatomy, physiology, psychology, and many interconnected medical terms.** On one occasion, you said,

"Why do we have heart, lungs, kidney? System is one, but each part has allotted day."

What is the context of this statement? How is it relevant to society? What message do you actually want to convey?

Swamy's Spirit Speaks:

Child, the human body is a **marvel of divine design.** It is not a collection of random organs but a **well-structured system where each part has a role to play, a function to perform, and a time to act.**

In the same way, **society is a larger body, a collective organism.** Just as different organs work together to sustain the body, different roles in society sustain the world. **Understand this deeper truth.**

1. **Context of the Statement:**

    *   The **heart, lungs, and kidneys do not work in isolation.** Each has its own function, yet they depend on one another.

    *   The **entire human system operates in harmony**, with each organ contributing at its own pace.

    *   Each part **has an "allotted day," meaning a time and purpose assigned to it**—when to function, when to rest, when to regenerate.

Similarly, **life has its phases, society has its roles, and every individual has a purpose.**

2. **Relevance to Society:**

◈ **One Society, Many Roles:**

Just as the body is one system with many organs, society is one system with many individuals—each with a unique contribution.

    *   A teacher educates.

    *   A doctor heals.

    *   A farmer nourishes.

    *   A leader guides.

All are essential, just like heart, lungs, and kidneys. No role is superior or inferior—**all must function in balance.**

◈ **Knowing Your Time and Function:**

- Just as the **heart beats continuously, lungs breathe rhythmically, and kidneys filter at intervals**, people must recognize their **own rhythm in life.**

- Some moments require action, some require patience.

- **A student must focus on learning before rushing to earn.**

- **A leader must listen before making decisions.**

- **A seeker must prepare before attaining wisdom.**

◈ **Overburdening Leads to Breakdown:**

- If **one organ takes on more than it can handle, the whole system collapses.**

- Similarly, in society, if individuals are **overburdened with stress, greed, or imbalance**, the collective structure suffers.

- **Greedy accumulation, unhealthy competition, and lack of rest disrupt the harmony of both body and society.**

◈ **Interdependence and Harmony:**

- No organ **functions alone**; it relies on the others.

- **No person thrives alone**; society must work together.

- **A balance between individuals, families, communities, and nations is needed.**

- Just as a **healthy body requires proper circulation, society needs the free flow of compassion, wisdom, and service.**

3. **The Deeper Message – What Swamy Wants to Convey:**

✔ **Understand that life is a system, not a competition.**

✔ **Recognize your role, perform it well, and allow others to do theirs.**

✔ **Do not rush or take on what is not yours—each has their time and place.**

✔ **Overworking, misusing energy, or disrupting balance leads to disease—both in the body and in society.**

✔ **Live in harmony, function with awareness, and support the system instead of burdening it.**

When each person understands their **purpose, time, and balance**, society will be as **healthy and synchronized as a perfectly functioning body.**

One system. Many parts. One harmony.

Chapter-73

Heart Circulates Life

The heart is not just the organ that pumps blood through our bodies; it symbolizes the very essence of life, connection, and vitality. Like a lifeline, the heart circulates energy, love, and purpose, sustaining not just our physical being but our spiritual essence as well. It is the centre from which emotions, intentions, and compassion flow, touching everyone and everything we encounter.

In the grand scheme of life, the heart is the source of boundless energy, guiding us toward empathy, understanding, and action. Just as the blood circulates through veins and arteries, our love, kindness, and care should circulate within us and outward to others, creating a ripple effect of positivity. When we nurture the heart—through compassion, gratitude, and mindfulness—we tap into the core of life's true power, elevating ourselves and the world around us. Let the heart lead, for it circulates life in its purest form.

** ** **

Swamy, in another context, you being a doctor mentioned and quoted:

"The heart gets blood. It does not manufacture blood. Its duty is to circulate."

This is so wonderful and correct, but what was the context in which you spoke these words? What message do you want to convey to society through this wisdom?

Swamy's Spirit Speaks:

Child, understand this **subtle truth**—the heart is not the creator of blood; it is merely a **distributor, a channel, a facilitator.** This principle applies not only to the **human body** but also to **life, knowledge, wealth, and wisdom.**

Many misunderstand their role in life. **People think they own what they receive, but in reality, they are just channels meant to circulate what is given to them.**

1. **Context of the Statement:**

    - The **heart is central** to the body, but it does not **create the blood** it pumps.

    - It **receives blood, oxygenates it, and ensures proper circulation** to every organ.

    - If the heart **hoards the blood** or **fails to circulate it properly**, the body collapses.

Similarly, in society:

    - **Wealth must circulate**—if hoarded, it leads to suffering.

    - **Knowledge must be shared**—if kept to oneself, it loses its value.

    - **Power must be used wisely**—if misused, it leads to oppression.

This understanding applies to **leaders, educators, professionals, and every human being.**

2. **Relevance to Society:**

◈ **Wealth and Resources Must Circulate:**

    - Just as the heart **receives blood and passes it on**, individuals who **earn wealth** must use it wisely—not hoard it.

    - **A society where wealth circulates benefits all.**

    - But when **a few hoard while others suffer, the entire system collapses—like a blocked artery leading to a heart attack.**

◈ **Knowledge Must Be Passed On:**

- A teacher, guru, or leader **must share their wisdom**—not keep it locked away.

- **What use is knowledge if it does not flow?**

- The duty of the wise is to **guide, uplift, and enlighten others.**

◈ **Love and Compassion Must Flow:**

- The **heart pumps blood selflessly**—it does not **favour one organ over another.**

- **Love, kindness, and service should be the same.**

- If you **restrict love, offer it selectively, or expect returns**, you disrupt the natural order.

◈ **Power Must Be Used for Service, Not Control:**

- **Leadership is not about hoarding power** but **circulating justice, fairness, and opportunities** for all.

- Just as the heart **ensures all parts receive blood**, a leader must ensure **every section of society thrives.**

3. **The Deeper Message – What Swamy Wants to Convey:**

✔ **You are not the creator; you are a channel.**

✔ **Receive, purify, and circulate—not hoard, misuse, or block.**

✔ **Understand that stagnation leads to decay, while movement sustains life.**

✔ **Circulation of wealth, knowledge, love, and service keeps society alive and healthy.**

✔ **A balanced life is one where giving and receiving flow in harmony.**

Just as the **heart never stops pumping until its last breath**, you too must continue to **serve, share, and uplift** without attachment or greed.

Be the heart that circulates goodness, not the blockage that leads to destruction.

Chapter-74

Assigned by Nature

Each one of us is born with a unique purpose, an assignment crafted by the universe itself. Nature, in its infinite wisdom, has designed us with strengths, talents, and passions that align perfectly with the greater flow of life. Our path may not always be clear, but deep within, we carry the blueprint of who we are meant to be.

Just as a seed is destined to grow into a tree, and a river is guided to find its course, our journey too is destined to unfold. Our choices, actions, and even challenges serve as part of the grand design, teaching us lessons and pushing us closer to fulfilling our true potential. In accepting our assignment, we align with the natural rhythm of existence, finding peace and purpose in our own journey.

When we trust in our place within the greater scheme of life, we stop resisting and start flowing with purpose. Nature has assigned us a role—be it as a nurturer, a creator, a healer, or a leader—and through each step, we contribute to the beautiful, interconnected web of life.

** ** **

Swamy, one of your quote states:

"Nature has allotted duties."

What do you want to communicate through this, especially from the perspective of society?

Swamy's Spirit Speaks:

Child, nature is **not random**; it functions in **perfect order**—every being, every element, and every force in creation has an **allotted duty**.

1. The Deeper Meaning – Nature's Design is Duty-Oriented

◈ **The Sun Rises and Sets Without Failing:**

- The **sun does not question its duty**; it **rises, gives light, nurtures life, and sets**—all without demand or complaint.

- It does not say, *"Today, I do not feel like rising!"*

◈ **The Rivers Flow Without Stopping:**

- A river **does not drink its own water**—it **flows to serve others.**

- It nourishes land, quenches thirst, and **moves forward**, never stagnant.

◈ **A Tree Bears Fruits for Others, Not Itself:**

- A tree **does not eat its own fruits.**

- It **gives shade, oxygen, and nourishment without asking, "What do I get in return?"**

◈ **Even the Smallest Creatures Have Duties:**

- **Bees pollinate flowers, ants clean the earth, cows give milk.**

- They do not **question their role**—they simply **fulfill their purpose in the grand design.**

2. How This Relates to Society

✔ **Every Being Has a Role to Play**

- **Parents** nurture and guide children.

- **Teachers** educate and shape young minds.

- **Leaders** serve and uplift society.

- **Farmers, doctors, engineers, artists—each has an allotted role.**

✔ **When Duties Are Performed Right, Society Thrives**

- If **leaders become selfish**, nations suffer.

- If **teachers do not teach properly**, knowledge declines.

- If **doctors forget their oath, health systems collapse.**

✔ **Problems Arise When Duties Are Ignored**

- The **sun does not refuse to shine**, but humans refuse to **fulfill their responsibilities.**

- **Greed, selfishness, and neglect of duty disturb the balance.**

3. **Swamy's Message – Living in Harmony with Duty**

🍃 **Perform Duty Without Ego** – Just as the **sun, rivers, and trees serve selflessly**, perform your duty with **dedication, not selfish motives.**

🍃 **Do Not Compare Duties** – A tree **does not ask why it is not the sun**, nor does the sun envy the moon. **Accept your role and do it well.**

🍃 **Understand That Duty is Beyond Professions** – A human's ultimate duty is to serve, uplift, and contribute to harmony.

🍃 **Balance Responsibility and Detachment** – Perform your duty, but do not get **attached to results.** A tree does not cry over **who eats its fruit.**

Final Thought – Nature's Example is the Best Teacher

◆ **The sun shines.**

◆ **The river flows.**

◆ **The tree gives.**

◈ **They do not complain, hesitate, or question their duty.**

◈ **Learn from them—do your duty, contribute, and create balance in society.**

A society that honours duty flourishes. A society that forgets duty **declines.**

Chapter-75

Synergistic Path

The Synergistic Path is one where individual strengths, efforts, and energies come together to create something greater than the sum of its parts. It's a journey of collaboration, where each step forward is fueled not just by personal ambition, but by the collective power of those around us. When we walk this path, we recognize that true growth happens when we support one another and align our intentions with the greater good.

On this path, we learn that our actions don't exist in isolation. Every decision, every interaction, and every choice we make reverberates through the collective, contributing to the larger web of life. The magic lies in the understanding that we are not separate from others, but intricately connected, and when we uplift each other, we all rise.

By embracing the Synergistic Path, we move beyond competition and scarcity, stepping into a space of abundance and shared success. It's a reminder that the more we come together in unity, the more powerful and transformative our journey becomes. Each individual's light contributes to a collective brilliance, guiding us toward a future filled with limitless potential.

Swamy, your explanation of **Karma, Bhakti, and Jnana** has been exceptional, and you linked them to **Dharma**. You once said:

"Karma: Do your duty, understand why.

Bhakti: Practicing the experience of Karma.

Jnana: The extension of Bhakti and Karma."

Although I have read numerous scriptures on these concepts, I prefer your divine wisdom to deepen my comprehension. Please explain.

Swamy's Spirit Speaks:

Child, the **journey of the soul** follows three stages—**Karma, Bhakti, and Jnana.** These are not **separate paths** but **interconnected steps** leading to the realization of truth.

1. Karma – The Path of Action:

◈ **Meaning:** *Karma is duty-bound action.*

◈ **Swamy's Words:** *"Do your duty, understand why."*

☑ **Action Without Awareness is Mere Labor:**

- A farmer **plows the field**—if he does not know **why** or **how**, his efforts go in vain.

- A teacher **teaches**—but **without understanding the purpose of education**, it remains mechanical.

- A doctor **treats patients**—but if he does it **only for money**, is it true Karma?

☑ **Duty Without Expectation:**

- Karma must be **done without attachment to rewards**.

- Like **a river flows without keeping water for itself**, **selfless action** is true Karma.

☑ **What Happens If Karma is Ignored?**

- A **student who does not study fails**.

- A **doctor who ignores his duty causes suffering**.

- A **leader who neglects responsibility weakens society**.

🕉 **"Karma is Dharma when performed with understanding."**

2. Bhakti – The Path of Devotion

◈ **Meaning:** *Bhakti is experiencing the divine through Karma.*

◈ **Swamy's Words:** *"Practicing the experience of Karma."*

✅ **Karma Done With Love Becomes Bhakti**

- A mother **cooking for her child with love** is Bhakti.

- A teacher **teaching with passion to uplift students** is Bhakti.

- A worker **serving society with dedication** is Bhakti.

✅ **How Bhakti Transforms Action**

- Bhakti **makes Karma meaningful and joyful**.

- Without Bhakti, **action is dry; with Bhakti, it becomes divine.**

✅ **Bhakti is Not Mere Rituals**

- It is **not just lighting lamps or singing hymns**.

- It is **surrendering ego and accepting the divine in all actions**.

🕉 **"When you offer your actions with devotion, Karma becomes Bhakti."**

3. Jnana – The Path of Knowledge

◈ **Meaning:** *Jnana is the realization of truth through Bhakti and Karma.*

◈ **Swamy's Words:** *"Jnana is the extension of Bhakti and Karma."*

✅ **When Devotion and Action Mature, Wisdom Arises**

- A **river starts as a small stream (Karma), gains depth (Bhakti), and merges into the ocean (Jnana).**

- A **student learns alphabets (Karma), understands their meaning (Bhakti), and finally realizes knowledge (Jnana).**

☑ Jnana is Seeing the Oneness in All

- A **wise person sees God in every action, every being, every moment.**

- He does not see **separation** between the self and the divine.

☑ What Happens If Jnana is Ignored?

- A **person may work (Karma) and pray (Bhakti) but without wisdom (Jnana), he remains confused.**

- Jnana is **clarity, enlightenment, and liberation from ignorance.**

🕉 **"Karma without Bhakti is dry. Bhakti without Jnana is blind. Jnana without Karma is incomplete."**

4. How They Link to Dharma

✔ **Karma aligns with Dharma** – Right action without selfishness.

✔ **Bhakti aligns with Dharma** – Devotion that purifies the heart.

✔ **Jnana aligns with Dharma** – Wisdom that reveals the eternal truth.

💡 **When all three are in harmony, life becomes Dharmic – purposeful, balanced, and fulfilling.**

Final Thought – Living with Karma, Bhakti, and Jnana

◈ **Act with duty (Karma).**

◈ **Love and surrender to the divine (Bhakti).**

◈ **Realize the ultimate truth (Jnana).**

🍃 **This is the journey from the human self to the divine self.**

🍃 **This is the secret of Dharma.**

🍃 **This is the key to liberation.**

Chapter-76

Open Heart

An open heart is the ultimate catalyst for meaningful connections, both with others and with ourselves. It's the art of embracing life's challenges with vulnerability, courage, and authenticity. When we open our hearts, we break down the walls of fear, pride, and judgment, allowing love and empathy to flow freely. It's not just about giving; it's about being open to receive, to experience life as it truly is—raw, beautiful, and ever-changing. An open heart is the foundation of deep relationships, for it's only when we allow ourselves to be fully present that we can truly understand and appreciate others.

Living with an open heart isn't always easy; it requires letting go of control, embracing uncertainty, and trusting in the process. But in doing so, we create a life that is rich with connection and purpose. It's about letting go of perfectionism, embracing our flaws, and finding strength in vulnerability. The more we open ourselves to the world with honesty and love, the more we invite meaningful experiences and genuine relationships into our lives.

On a spiritual level, an open heart is the gateway to infinite growth and wisdom. It allows us to tap into a deeper sense of connection with the divine, guiding us on a path of peace, compassion, and self-discovery. When we live from the heart, we unlock a powerful flow of universal energy that transforms not just our own lives, but the lives of those we touch. An open heart is a channel for grace, love, and healing—bringing light to the world in ways we can't even begin to measure.

Swamy, you once said,

"If you expose, you could be explored; express your inner feelings, then you extend."

I understand the general essence of these words, but I feel that some intricate links are missing in my understanding. Could you please share your wisdom and explain the deeper meaning behind this statement so that I may grasp its full significance?

Swamy's Spirit Speaks:

Child, these words are an invitation to embark on a journey of self-revelation and authentic expression—a process that leads to the natural expansion of your inner light. Let me break down the deeper layers for you:

- **"If you expose":**

  This is a call to open your heart and reveal your true self without fear. To expose means to let go of the masks that hide your inner essence, allowing your vulnerabilities and truths to shine forth.

  - When you courageously expose your inner self, you invite honest introspection and self-awareness.

- **"You could be explored":**

  Once you have exposed your true self, you become open to exploration—both by yourself and by those who encounter you.

  - This exploration is not a superficial examination; it is a deep dive into the soul, uncovering hidden strengths, lessons, and potentials.

  - It is through this exploration that you learn more about who you are and what you are capable of, enriching your understanding of life.

- **"Express your inner feelings":**

  With your inner self exposed and explored, you are then able to articulate your genuine emotions and insights.

  - This expression is not mere chatter, but a heartfelt communication of your true essence.

  - When you express your inner feelings with honesty and clarity, you not only free yourself but also inspire others to connect with their own truth.

- **"Then you extend":**

  Finally, this authentic expression naturally extends your energy, love, and wisdom into the world.

  - Extension means sharing your inner light, thereby expanding the positive influence you have on others.

  - As you extend your authentic self, you create a ripple effect, uplifting those around you and contributing to a more harmonious collective consciousness.

In essence, the process is a graceful cycle:

Expose your true self → **Explore** the depths of your inner being → **Express** your heartfelt truth → **Extend** your transformed energy to the world.

Child, this cycle is the path to personal and spiritual growth. It is not about mere self-disclosure but about a transformative journey that leads to deeper self-knowledge and a more profound connection with the Divine and with others.

May you always have the courage to be vulnerable, the wisdom to seek deeper truths, and the compassion to share your authentic self, so that your inner light may extend and inspire all.

Chapter-77

Collective Harmony

Collective harmony is the energy that arises when individuals come together with a shared purpose, vision, and intention, creating a powerful force that is greater than the sum of its parts. It is the collective rhythm of a group—whether family, community, or society—working in unison to create a space where peace, understanding, and love thrive. Just as an orchestra functions best when every instrument is in tune and plays its part, collective harmony arises when each person contributes their unique gifts and energies to the whole. When we operate in harmony, we are able to achieve remarkable things together that would be impossible alone.

At its core, collective harmony is about understanding that we are all connected. Every thought, word, and action has a ripple effect that impacts the collective energy. When individuals align their energies with love, respect, and compassion, the entire group thrives. This requires us to transcend ego, judgment, and division, recognizing that our differences are not a source of conflict but an opportunity for growth and learning. Collective harmony is about finding common ground, celebrating diversity, and fostering an environment where everyone feels valued and heard.

Spiritually, collective harmony is rooted in the belief that we are all expressions of a higher divine energy. When we unite in a space of shared intention, we tap into this universal energy and allow it to guide and uplift us. It is through collective harmony that we experience the true power of oneness. In moments of true unity, we transcend the limitations of the individual and become vessels for divine flow. This spiritual connection fosters peace, compassion, and understanding among all, creating an environment where the divine presence is felt in every action and every interaction.

In a world that often feels divided, collective harmony reminds us of the power of unity and the strength that comes from collaboration. It is through collective harmony that we heal, grow, and evolve—not just as individuals, but as a collective force capable of making a profound difference in the world. When we align ourselves with this energy, we become active participants in creating a world filled with peace, love, and prosperity for all.

**** ** ****

Swamy, you often speak,

"Ego, selfishness should go, then only society will improve."

Yet, in this Kaliyuga—an age marked by modernity that makes minds complex, rampant competition among nations, communities, castes, and religions, and where humanity seems lost—how is it possible to overcome ego and selfishness? What solution do you suggest, and what role do the Peetadhipatis play in this regard?

Swamy's Spirit Speaks:

Child, the challenge of dissolving ego and selfishness in this turbulent age is immense, yet the timeless wisdom of inner transformation remains the beacon that can lead society toward harmony. Let me explain the deeper essence of this teaching:

- **The Root of Conflict:**

  Ego and selfishness are the seeds of division. They blind you to the unity of all existence, compelling you to act out of fear, competition, and desire for control. When each individual clings to a limited sense of self, collective well-being is sacrificed for personal gain.

- **Possibility in Kaliyuga:**

  Although modernity and complexity seem to magnify these challenges, the path to transcending ego lies in the individual. Each person, through sincere self-awareness, disciplined practice, and a willingness to embrace humility, can gradually dissolve these barriers.

  - **Inner transformation** is the antidote to the external chaos; when you change from within, the world around you begins to change as well.

- **The Role of Inner Transformation:**

  Begin by turning your attention inward. Through meditation, self-reflection, and mindful service, you can overcome the pull of ego and selfishness.

  - When you liberate your mind and heart from the constraints of personal desire, you open yourself to a higher, universal truth that sees all beings as interconnected.

  - This shift in consciousness not only enriches your own life but also radiates outwards, encouraging others to follow a similar path.

- **The Role of Peetadhipatis (Spiritual Leaders):**

  Peetadhipatis serve as guiding lights in these challenging times. They are the custodians of spiritual heritage who, by embodying a life free of ego and selfishness, inspire others to awaken to their higher potential.

  - Their teachings help you see beyond the immediate allure of material success and competitive rivalry, pointing you toward a life of compassion, unity, and selfless service.

  - By offering wisdom, support, and practical guidance, they help create environments where inner transformation is not only possible but actively nurtured.

- **The Broader Solution:**

  The transformation of society begins with the transformation of the individual. While the external world may be mired in competition and division, every act of inner awakening contributes to a larger ripple of positive change.

  - **Cultivate Inner Peace:** Let each person work on shedding ego and embracing compassion.

  - **Foster Community Dialogue:** Create spaces where genuine, non-competitive dialogue and mutual support are the norms.

  - **Embrace Collective Responsibility:** Recognize that every small step toward selflessness adds to the collective upliftment of society.

Child, while it may seem that the external forces of modernity conspire to deepen divisions, the true change is seeded within the heart. When you and others strive to overcome ego and selfishness, you contribute to a higher order—a society where unity, love, and cooperation flourish.

May you find the strength to embark on this inner journey, and may the divine grace of the Peetadhipatis and the eternal wisdom guide you toward a future of harmonious living.

Chapter-78

Aspiring Inspiration

Aspiring inspiration is the inner spark that propels us toward growth, creativity, and transformation. It is the force that encourages us to rise above limitations, seek higher understanding, and strive for greatness, even in the face of adversity. Inspiration isn't just an external force—it is deeply rooted within us, waiting to be awakened and channelled into purposeful action.

At its core, aspiring inspiration is about connecting with our highest potential and aligning our efforts with a greater purpose. It invites us to expand our horizons, not just through external achievements, but by nurturing our inner light. This drive inspires us to seek knowledge, serve others, and create a lasting impact in the world.

In the spiritual context, aspiring inspiration is the constant reminder that we are divinely supported in our journey toward self-realization. It encourages us to embrace challenges as opportunities for growth, and to trust that the universe provides the necessary guidance to fulfill our destiny.

When we cultivate aspiring inspiration, we not only shape our future but also contribute to the collective energy of humanity, igniting a wave of transformation and enlightenment.

** ** **

Swamy, you once said,

"Aspire to inspire before you expire."

Your words carry a strong and compelling message, and I would like to understand it more deeply. Could you kindly clarify what you mean by this and how one can practically embody this principle in life?

Swamy's Spirit Speaks:

Child, these words are a call to live with purpose and leave a lasting, positive impact on the world. Let me share the inner essence behind this message:

- **"Aspire to Inspire":**

  - **Aspire** means to set lofty goals, to dream boldly, and to strive relentlessly for excellence. It is a commitment to evolving your inner self and expanding your vision beyond the mundane.

  - **Inspire** means to radiate your inner light in such a way that others are uplifted, encouraged, and motivated to embark on their own journey of growth and transformation. When you live authentically and with passion, your very presence becomes a beacon for those around you.

- **"Before You Expire":**

  - Life is transient, and every moment is precious. The phrase reminds you that time is limited, so the opportunity to make a difference is now.

  - Rather than postponing your aspirations or waiting for an ideal moment that may never come, you must act in the present.

  - It urges you not to let your life slip by unnoticed, but to invest your time and energy in creating a legacy of positive influence.

- **Practical Steps to Embody This Principle:**

  - **Live with Purpose:**

    - Identify your deepest values and passions. Let them guide your actions every day.

    - When you align your life with your true purpose, you naturally inspire others to seek their own truth.

- **Share Your Journey:**
  - Be open about your struggles, triumphs, and the lessons you learn along the way.
  - Your authentic story can serve as a guiding light for others, showing them that transformation is possible.

- **Practice Compassion and Generosity:**
  - Small acts of kindness can create ripples of inspiration.
  - Help others whenever you can—whether through mentorship, encouragement, or simply by offering a listening ear.

- **Cultivate Inner Excellence:**
  - Continuously strive to improve yourself—emotionally, mentally, and spiritually.
  - By nurturing your own growth, you become a living example of what it means to pursue a higher purpose.

- **Seize Every Moment:**
  - Embrace each day as a unique opportunity to leave your mark on the world.
  - Remember that even the smallest positive action, when done consistently, contributes to a larger legacy.

- **The Ultimate Message:**

  Child, "Aspire to inspire before you expire" is a call to live with urgency and integrity. It is a reminder that your life, though finite, has infinite potential if you use your time wisely. When you commit to your highest ideals and share your inner brilliance, you not only transform yourself but also kindle the spark of hope and possibility in others.

May you always find the courage to pursue your dreams with passion, and may your life shine as a testament to the power of inspiration.

Chapter-79

Begging Beyond

In life, we often ask for what we think we lack, believing that we are in need of something beyond ourselves. But Begging Beyond is about recognizing that we don't need to beg for anything external. Instead, it's about turning inward and realizing that the Divine Mother is already within us, guiding and nurturing us every moment.

When we turn to the Mother, we do not ask out of desperation but out of devotion. Begging implies a sense of emptiness, but in truth, we are never truly lacking. The Mother is always with us, and our prayers should not be pleas for something we don't have, but an offering of our heart, a call to connect with her divine presence inside us.

And yet, when challenges arise, when life feels harsh, we may wonder why we are being tested. But these challenges are not punishments. They are the Mother's way of shaping us, helping us grow. The strikes we feel are not meant to hurt us, but to refine us. These are moments of purification, where we are being molded into something stronger, wiser, and more aligned with our true selves.

Begging Beyond is about moving past the idea that we are lacking something. It's about trusting that the Divine is already within us and that whatever we face is part of our spiritual growth. We stop begging for answers and start accepting the wisdom that life, through the Mother, brings us. Even in difficult moments, there is grace. Every challenge is a lesson. Every strike is a step toward greater understanding.

Ultimately, Begging Beyond is about letting go of the need to ask for things we think we need. Instead, we begin to recognize what's already here—within us and around us. It's about moving from a place of longing to one of knowing, from asking for more to recognizing the divine gifts we already possess.

**** ** ****

During our recent conversation, you told me, "Don't beg, don't get beaten up."

Who else can I turn to but the Cosmic Mother? I will not ask for what is undesired, for I understand what nurtures my soul and sustains my physical being. It is only to strengthen myself in His gaze that I invoke the sacred names of Rama and Krishna, seeking purity.

But tell me, Swamy, is asking the Mother the same as begging? Then why did she strike me? Even if she does, she remains my Mother, and I accept it. Yet, I long to grasp the spiritual essence behind your words. My heart whispers a meaning, but I seek confirmation from you.

Child, you asked, 'Don't beg, don't get beaten up'. A powerful question, for it strikes at the heart of how we relate to the Divine. Imagine for a moment that the Mother is not far from you, but lives within you, in every thought, every action, every heartbeat. She is not somewhere distant, waiting to answer your pleas. She is the very fabric of your being. So, to ask her is not to beg, but to remember that she is already present, waiting for you to realize her presence.

When I say 'Don't beg', I mean don't approach the Divine from a place of weakness. Don't reduce yourself to a beggar at the gates of the universe. You are not in need of what you think you are lacking. The Divine doesn't deal in the currency of begging. Instead, approach with confidence—knowing that you are part of the Divine whole. Ask not from a place of emptiness, but from a space of fullness, trusting that the Divine knows what your soul truly needs, even if it doesn't match your immediate desires.

Now, why does the Mother 'beat' you? This is where the mystery lies. She is not beating you out of anger, but out of love, the kind of love that is unafraid to challenge you, to shake you awake from the slumber of attachment. The beatings are not for punishment—they are for transformation. In your discomfort, in your confusion, you are being shaped into someone capable of standing in her presence, unshaken by life's storms. The pain is her way of breaking the shell, so that the true self, the soul, can emerge.

So, is it begging to ask the Mother for guidance? No. But what you must realize is that the act of asking is not one of external pleading, but a call for internal clarity. It is not about what the world gives you, but what you awaken within yourself. You do not beg for her love, you awaken it. You do not beg for her presence, you recognize it. The Mother isn't someone you go to for something outside you. She is the very force that makes you you—your challenges, your wisdom, your joy, your growth.

Even if the Mother seems to 'strike' you, know this: It is her way of lovingly guiding you to see the hidden truths within. When you feel the sting, know that it is her grace at work, guiding you closer to who you are meant to be. You do not need to beg, because you are already in her embrace. You need only to recognize it."

Chapter-80

Rising Beyond Self

When life shatters your world, it is not the end—it is the beginning of something far greater than you can yet see. Collapse is the divine's way of clearing the path, stripping away illusions, and dismantling all that is built on fear, attachment, and false identity. In the wreckage of what once was, a deeper truth emerges. You may feel lost, but in reality, you are being found. You are being prepared, refined, and realigned with your higher purpose. The pain that seems unbearable is not here to destroy you—it is here to awaken you.

But awakening is incomplete without action. True transformation happens when you take what life has taught you and offer it to the world. Your suffering is not meaningless; it carries the seeds of wisdom, compassion, and strength. Rise, not just for yourself, but for those who walk the same path. Let your wounds become a source of healing, your struggles a source of guidance. This is the sacred cycle of existence: to fall, to rise, to give. Walk forward with faith, for the divine does not dwell in the past but in the endless unfolding of what is yet to be.

** ** **

Swamy suddenly called me, lost in recollection, his voice heavy with memories of his youth—a time filled with dreams yet shadowed by the devastating loss of four loved ones at once: his father, mother, grandmother, and grandfather. He admitted that these memories still resurface, unsettling his mind. Then, in a moment of profound clarity, he said, **"Collide, Collapse, Conceive, Contribute—Go forward, but never backwards."**

Swamy, I, too, have endured deep trauma—the painful loss of my sister, brother, and parents, one after another. When I asked you how you found the strength to move forward despite such unbearable sorrow, you said, **"The Mystic Energy carried me."** Life is an enigma, full of uninvited storms that drain our very essence. And yet, it moves forward, urging us to do the same. I need you to explain the intention behind using such words.

Swamy's Spirit Speaks:

My child, you ask what I mean by these words. This is not mere philosophy but the essence of life's divine movement. Do you seek clarity? Let the great ones who walked before you in our sacred epics illuminate the path.

Collide, Collapse, Conceive, Contribute—Go Forward, Never Backward:

Collide—The Unavoidable Impact

"Life does not wait for your readiness. It strikes. It shakes. It collides with your illusions, your expectations, your comforts. You will meet loss, suffering, betrayal, and uncertainty. Do not resist. Collision is necessary. It is the divine knocking at your door, asking you to awaken. You are not here to escape suffering—you are here to face it, understand it, and transcend it."

◈ Example from the Epics: Arjuna at Kurukshetra. The great warrior collides with an unbearable reality—the duty to fight against his own kin. He is shattered, overcome by doubt and despair. But in that collision, Krishna's wisdom awakens him to the truth beyond illusion.

Collapse—The Breaking Down of What Was:

"When the storm is strong, the weak structures within you will collapse. Let them. Collapse is not failure; it is purification. The false self, the attachments, the illusions—they must fall away. In this moment, you may feel helpless, lost, and shattered. Do not fear. The universe never destroys without purpose. Collapse is the beginning of true transformation."

◈ Example from the Epics: King Harishchandra, whose kingdom, wealth, and even family were taken from him. He collapsed into nothingness, reduced to a crematorium keeper. But in that collapse, he shed all ego, and his truthfulness led him to ultimate liberation.

Conceive—The Birth of Inner Sight:

"From the ashes of collapse, something new is conceived. A deeper understanding, a new vision, a strength you did not know you had. This is when you begin to see—not with your eyes, but with your soul. You realize that suffering was never meant to break you; it was meant to birth you anew. The pain you endured now reveals its purpose: to expand your awareness beyond what you once thought possible."

◈ Example from the Epics: Prahlada, the young child devotee of Lord Vishnu. Despite being tortured by his father, he conceived a higher truth—that the divine is omnipresent. His suffering gave birth to unwavering faith, which even death could not shake.

Contribute—The Sacred Offering of the Self:

"What will you do with this realization? Will you keep it locked inside, or will you share it? True healing comes not from holding wisdom but from giving it. The wounds you carry are not just yours; they are the wounds of many. Let your suffering become your offering. Serve. Guide. Illuminate. Give back to the world what pain once took from you. This is the purpose of every awakened soul—to contribute, to uplift, to heal."

◈ Example from the Epics: Karna, the son of the Sun God. Despite rejection and suffering, he chose to contribute his strength to the world. He gave away everything—even his life—without hesitation. His generosity was his highest dharma.

Go Forward—Flow with the Eternal Current:

"Life moves in one direction—forward. There is no returning to what was, no undoing of what has been. The past is a lesson, not a destination. Carry its wisdom, but do not cling to its weight. Keep walking, keep growing, keep expanding. The river does not flow backward, nor should you. Every step forward is a step closer to truth, to peace, to the divine."

◈ Example from the Epics: Rama, after exile, loss, and war, did not turn back. He walked the path of dharma unwaveringly, understanding that duty lies ahead, not behind.

Never Backward—For the Divine Is Ahead, Not Behind:

"Do not look back in longing or regret. What has left you was never truly yours. What is ahead is where you are meant to be. Trust. Surrender. Walk on. The mystic energy that moves the stars and the seas is the same force that moves you. Let it carry you beyond pain, beyond fear, beyond yourself. The journey is not to return to who you were—it is to become who you are destined to be."

◈ Example from the Epics: Draupadi, after suffering humiliation, loss, and exile, did not dwell in the past. She moved forward with the Pandavas, embracing destiny and ensuring justice prevailed.

Final Words of Swamy's Spirit

"When life collides with you, do not fear.

When you collapse, do not despair.

When you conceive a new vision, trust it.

When you contribute, give from the depth of your being.

And above all, move forward; always move forward.

For the divine does not dwell in what is lost but in what is yet to be found.

This is the way. Walk it."

THE VASTNESS WITHIN

(Discovering Infinite Potential Within and aligning
with universal intelligence)

Chapter-81

Anchoring Stillness in Life's Turbulence

Stillness is not about silencing the world around you; it is about finding an unshakable centre within. Life will always bring waves of uncertainty—memories from the past, fears of the future, and challenges in the present. Yet, just as the ocean's depths remain undisturbed despite surface storms, true stillness lies in going deeper within yourself. It is not about avoiding emotions or struggles but about watching them without being consumed by them.

To cultivate this stillness, one must learn to let go—of resistance, of control, of the need to grasp or push away. Imagine a river that flows effortlessly around obstacles, never stopping, never struggling. In the same way, when we surrender to life's rhythm instead of fighting against it, we find clarity, peace, and the strength to move forward without losing ourselves.

Swamy, you often emphasize the importance of inner stillness, yet I find it oscillating, leaving me unsettled. Physical ailments disrupt this balance, past memories bring haunting pain, and the future feels uncertain. How can one cultivate and sustain true stillness amidst such turbulence? Is there a path to achieving it?

**** ** ****

Swamy's Spirit Answers: Anchoring Stillness Amidst Life's Turbulence:

My child, stillness wavers when the mind clings to what was or fears what may be.

Stillness is not something that disappears—it is only overshadowed by the restless mind. When you hold on to the pain of the past or anxiously anticipate the future, your mind oscillates between suffering and worry. Imagine a candle in a room with open windows. The wind from the past and future keeps it flickering. But when you close those windows, the flame remains steady.

A person who has experienced great loss may feel trapped in sorrow, constantly reliving painful memories. Another may dread the future, fearing what is yet to come. Both lose their inner peace because their minds are caught in time—either behind or ahead—but never in the present moment.

The body may ache, memories may stir, and the future may seem unclear—but you are not these passing clouds; you are the sky.

Pain, thoughts, and emotions are like clouds passing through the vast sky of your awareness. Sometimes the sky is stormy; other times, it is clear. But the sky itself is untouched by the clouds. Similarly, your true self—pure awareness—remains unaffected by life's fleeting difficulties.

Consider a monk sitting in meditation despite physical pain. He acknowledges the discomfort but does not let it define him. A person grieving may feel sorrow, but when they understand that emotions come and go like waves, they no longer drown in them. They become the observer rather than the sufferer.

Breathe, observe, and let go. The river does not fight the current; it flows. Be the flow, not the resistance.

The key to maintaining stillness is not to resist life's changes but to flow with them. When you resist pain, it intensifies. When you fear the unknown, it becomes heavier. But when you allow yourself to observe, accept, and move with life rather than against it, peace naturally follows.

A wise farmer does not curse the seasons but adapts to them. A wise mind does not cling to suffering but flows with life's rhythm. Just as the river does not fight obstacles but moves around them, learn to embrace life's experiences without attachment or fear. That is where stillness is found.

Chapter-82

Walking in the Light of the Rishis

To walk in the light of the Rishis is to walk with wisdom as your guide, truth as your foundation, and selflessness as your path. The Rishis were not bound by time or place; their reflections still shine in the silent depths of those who seek the eternal. Their wisdom is not mere knowledge but a living force—felt in the stillness of meditation, in the purity of thought, and in the compassion of action. To align with their light is to transform life itself into a sacred offering, where every word carries truth, every action radiates love, and every moment becomes a step toward the infinite.

When we truly absorb their reflections, life ceases to be a struggle and becomes a harmonious flow. The burdens of ego dissolve, and a deeper purpose unfolds—not in seeking, but in becoming. The one who walks in their light does not need to preach, for their very presence uplifts. Such a being is like a river that nourishes without expectation, like the morning sun that awakens without command. In the footsteps of the Rishis, we do not merely exist—we illuminate.

** ** **

Swamy, you often emphasize that spiritual aspirants should be under the reflections of the Rishis.

1. **What do you truly mean by the "reflections of Rishis"?** Are these reflections their teachings, their way of life, or something beyond words?

2. **How can one come under these reflections?** Is it through scriptures, meditation, or an inner connection with their wisdom?

3. **In what ways does this benefit both the soul and society?** Does the transformation of an individual naturally lead to the upliftment of the world?

4. **How can one cultivate these reflections in daily life?** Are there signs to recognize if we are truly absorbing and living their wisdom?

Swamy, please guide me on how to walk this path and embody the essence of the Rishis in thought, word, and action.

Dear child,

The *reflections of the Rishis* are not just their words or actions but the very essence of their realized wisdom—timeless, boundless, and ever-radiant. To be under their reflections means to align your mind, heart, and soul with the higher truths they embodied. It is not mere study; it is an absorption, a transformation, a surrender to the eternal light they carried.

How does one come under these reflections? Not by seeking them outside, but by tuning inward. The Rishis did not leave behind mere teachings; they left a vibration, a living presence, accessible to those who seek with sincerity. Through deep contemplation, selfless action, and unwavering truthfulness, you invite their presence into your life. When your thoughts are pure, when your words uplift, when your actions serve—know that the Rishis are reflecting through you.

When this reflection takes root, both the soul and society are illuminated. The soul finds its rightful path, free from confusion, anchored in divine wisdom. Society, in turn, is uplifted—not by force, but by the silent radiance of a transformed being. Just as a lamp does not declare its light but dispels darkness by its very nature, one who reflects the Rishis becomes a beacon without effort.

How do you know if you are truly under their reflection? Observe yourself. Do your thoughts carry clarity? Do your words carry truth? Do your actions carry compassion? If so, the Rishis are within you, their wisdom flowing through your every breath. Live in such a way that their presence is felt—not in temples or scriptures alone, but in the way you move, the way you serve, the way you love.

Child, walk this path with sincerity, and soon you will realize—you are not just under their reflection; you *are* their reflection.

LIVING BEYOND BOUNDARIES

(Integrating Expanded Awareness into Daily Life)

Chapter-83

Realization Flows as Service

When the Self is truly realized, service ceases to be an act and becomes a natural flow—like a river that does not decide whom to nourish or the sun that does not choose whom to shine upon. In the light of realization, the false divisions of 'I' and 'you' dissolve, revealing a profound truth: to serve others is to serve the Self, for there is no other. The hands that uplift, the words that heal, and the heart that loves are not separate from the divine presence that moves through all.

True service is not bound by duty or expectation; it is the silent offering of a soul that has touched the infinite. It does not seek recognition, nor is it weighed down by the need for results. It flows effortlessly—like a fragrance from a blooming flower, like waves returning to the shore. In such service, there is no giver and no receiver, only the joyous unfolding of realization in action.

Swamy, you often emphasize Self-Realization and Service, describing it as Realization in Action. I would like to gain a deeper understanding of these concepts.

1. What do you mean by "Self"? Is it the physical body, the mind, the soul, or something beyond all these?

2. What is "Realization"? Is it an intellectual understanding, an experiential awakening, or a state of being?

3. How do you define "Service"? Is it limited to helping others, or does it encompass something more profound?

4. How are Self-Realization and Service interconnected? Does true service emerge as a natural outcome of Self-Realization, or is service itself a path to realizing the Self?

Could you please elaborate on these aspects and guide me on how one can embody this Realization in Action in everyday life?

Dear child,

You seek to understand *Self-Realization* and *Service*, the essence of *Realization in Action*. Listen carefully.

1. **What is the Self?**

   The Self is not the body, nor the mind, nor the fleeting emotions. It is the eternal, unchanging awareness—the witness behind all experiences. It is neither bound by birth nor death, untouched by sorrow or joy. The Self is the very source of existence, beyond name and form.

2. **What is Realization?**

   Realization is not mere knowledge; it is awakening to the truth of who you are. It is the moment when the illusion of separateness dissolves, and you see the universe as an extension of your own being. This is not an intellectual conclusion but a direct, undeniable experience—like a river realizing it was never separate from the ocean.

3. **What is Service?**

   Service is not an act of charity; it is the expression of the realized Self. When you recognize that the same divine presence pervades all, service ceases to be an obligation—it becomes your very nature. A lamp does not shine for itself; its light is for others. The truly realized one serves effortlessly, without seeking recognition, without expectation, like the sun giving warmth to all.

4. **How are Self-Realization and Service connected?**

   Realization without service is incomplete, and service without realization lacks depth. When you truly know the Self, you see no distinction between yourself and others. Their hunger becomes your hunger, their suffering your own. In that moment, service is not something you *do*—it is what you *are*.

Child, *Realization in Action* means living in the awareness of this oneness. It is seeing the divine in all, moving through life with compassion, and acting with selflessness. It is not renouncing the world, but embracing it with wisdom and love.

Walk this path with sincerity, and in time, you will see—there is no difference between the one who serves, the one who is served, and the act of service itself.

Chapter-84

Awakened Leadership

Awakened leadership is not about power, position, or control—it is about radiating wisdom, embodying truth, and serving selflessly. A true leader is not one who divides but one who dissolves differences, not one who commands but one who inspires. India, with its vast spiritual heritage, has always been guided by such enlightened beings—visionaries who saw beyond caste, creed, and boundaries, embracing all as one. From Adi Shankaracharya, who traversed the land to unify diverse spiritual traditions, to Swami Vivekananda, who awakened national pride through the message of inner strength, their leadership was rooted in Dharma, in service, in awakening the highest potential within all.

Today, as India rises on the global stage, the call for awakened leadership is more urgent than ever. A leader must be a bridge, not a barrier—a unifier who uplifts society with wisdom, compassion, and unwavering commitment to truth. In a world of rapid change, where distractions and divisions seek to weaken the spirit of unity, the true leader must stand as an anchor, reminding us of our shared heritage, our common destiny. When leadership is infused with spiritual awareness, action becomes selfless, governance becomes righteous, and society flourishes in harmony. This is the leadership that India needs—the leadership that does not merely lead but enlightens, that does not seek to rule but to serve.

** ** **

Swamy, the great Peetadhipathis (Pontiff), embodies awakened leadership—where silence speaks and actions resonate. In today's increasingly divisive world, which struggles with inclusivity, what role do they truly need to play? How does their leadership manifest in such times, and under what circumstances does meaningful transformation take place? Is there a deeper, unseen force that connects them all in fulfilling a higher, noble purpose?

The Spirit of Swamy Answers:

"A true leader is not confined by boundaries but expands into limitless awareness. In times of division, their presence itself becomes a guiding force—bringing harmony where there is discord and clarity where there is confusion. Peetadhipathis have the sacred responsibility to uphold Dharma, not by imposing, but by inspiring, not by controlling, but by uniting.

History has shown that when darkness clouds the minds of people, awakened souls emerge as guiding lights. Sri Adi Shankaracharya traversed the length and breadth of Bharat to re-establish the wisdom of Advaita, not through force, but by sheer clarity of thought and the radiance of his presence. Swami Vivekananda, with just a few words, ignited a spiritual awakening in the West, not by seeking followers but by reminding humanity of its innate divinity. Similarly, Mahatma Gandhi's leadership was not one of authority but of moral strength—his silence often spoke louder than words, and his nonviolent resistance shook the foundations of oppressive rule.

Sanatana Dharma, the eternal path, is not just a philosophy of the past but a living, breathing guide to navigating the complexities of the modern world. Rooted in universal principles of righteousness (Dharma), selfless action (Karma), and inner realization (Jnana), it offers a framework for inclusivity, sustainability, and harmony. In a time when societies are fragmented by differences, Sanatana Dharma reminds us that all paths lead to the same truth and that real leadership lies in recognizing the oneness that underlies all existence. By integrating its wisdom, today's leaders can transcend divisions and cultivate a world guided by consciousness, compassion, and collective well-being.

Today, Peetadhipathis (Pontiff) has a unique opportunity to be the guiding force that society needs. By embracing their role as unifiers, they can uplift people beyond differences and awaken a shared sense of purpose. Through wisdom, compassion, and unwavering commitment to truth, they can inspire a new era of harmony and higher consciousness. And yes, a divine thread connects all awakened souls—the silent call of selfless service, the unwavering resolve of truth, and the boundless grace of Dharma. When these forces align, the world naturally moves toward greater unity, understanding, and spiritual awakening.

Chapter-85

Invisible Impact

True service does not seek recognition; it flows silently, shaping lives and transforming societies in unseen ways. In a world driven by visibility, the power of selfless action often goes unnoticed, yet its impact is profound. Every small act of kindness, every moment of mindful work, contributes to a greater ripple in the cosmos. The challenge lies in initiating this journey—understanding that service is not just about charity but about making every action meaningful. Accomplishing it requires dedication, consistency, and a heart free from expectations. With its energy and innovation, the present generation has a vital role in carrying this forward. By integrating compassion into daily life, they can become the unseen hands that move the world toward harmony and transformation.

** ** **

Swamy, you often speak of "Invisible Impact". In a world where recognition matters, do unseen acts of kindness and service still shape our lives and society? If every action, big or small, leaves an impact, how can we make our daily work more meaningful? How do we begin this journey of selfless service, and what does it take to accomplish it with true dedication? What role does today's youth play in carrying forward this spirit of sacred action in a fast-changing world?

The Spirit of Swamy Speaks:

True service is like a gentle breeze—it moves without seeking attention, yet its presence can be felt everywhere. In today's world, where recognition often takes centre stage, do silent acts of kindness still matter? The answer lies in the way unseen hands have always shaped society—through selfless actions, quiet sacrifices, and a deep sense of duty that expects nothing in return. Every action, whether big or small, carries energy. What truly matters is the intention behind it.

Making our daily work meaningful does not require grand gestures; it begins with small, sincere efforts. A kind word, a helping hand, or simply doing one's duty with dedication are the building blocks of a life serving a higher purpose. The journey of selfless service starts when we shift our focus from 'What do I gain?' to 'How can I contribute?' To accomplish this, we need patience, consistency, and the wisdom to see service not as a burden but as a natural expression of inner growth.

Today's youth have the power to redefine service in ways never seen before. With their energy, innovation, and global reach, they can integrate compassion into technology, leadership, and everyday life. It is not about unthinking old traditions but about awakening to the spirit of sacred action in a way that aligns with the modern world. When young minds act with selflessness and purpose, they become the invisible force that shapes the future—moving the world towards unity, peace, and true progress.

Today's youth hold the key to redefining service in ways that were once unimaginable. With their boundless energy, innovative mindset, and unprecedented global connectivity, they have the ability to weave compassion into the very fabric of technology, leadership, and daily life. True service is not about unthinkingly following traditions but awakening to a deeper sense of purpose that harmonizes ancient wisdom with modern realities. When young minds rise above self-interest and dedicate themselves to meaningful action, they transform into a silent yet powerful force, shaping a future built on unity, peace, and lasting progress.

www.ingramcontent.com/pod-product-compliance
Lightning Source LLC
Chambersburg PA
CBHW060517160726
47991CB00001B/76